The Polk Street Review

a celebration of Noblesville, Indiana

The Polk Street Review

2019 edition

If I Only Knew Then What I Know Now . . .

published by

Logan Street Sanctuary Press

EST. 2017

2019

First Printing: 2019

Participating Authors, Photographers, Artists, and Musicians retain all copyrights to their material; all material used with permission.

Cover design: Alys Caviness-Gober
Cover art: Old Mill & Grain Elevator: Alys Caviness-Gober
Project management, formatting, and layout: Alys Caviness-Gober
Editors: Alys Caviness-Gober & Sarah E. Morin
Back cover design: Alys Caviness-Gober

ISBN-13: 978-0-9998858-2-6

Logan Street Sanctuary Press
a division of Logan Street Sanctuary, Inc.
1274 Logan Street
Noblesville, IN 46060
1st Printing: February 2019
http://loganstreetsanctuary.org

Ordering Information:
Special discounts are available on quantity purchases by corporations, associations, educators, and others. Please contact Alys at loganstreetsanctuary@gmail.com for details.
U.S. trade bookstores and wholesalers: please contact Alys at loganstreetsanctuary@gmail.com for details.

Dedicated to
our community,
our friends,
and
our families

2019 Logan Street Sanctuary, Inc. Acknowledgements

Logan Street Sanctuary, Inc. (LSS) is a recipient of operational support grants from the Hamilton County Community Foundation and Hamilton County Tourism, and the 2019 edition of *The Polk Street Review* received an Indiana Arts Commission FY2019 Project Support grant award. LSS partners with and receives support from several organizations and businesses. This book, and everything we do, would not be possible without the help of these wonderful organizations and businesses.

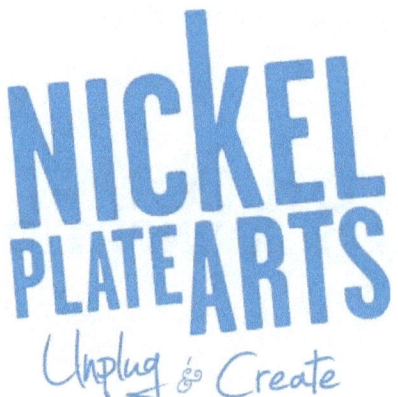

Sacred Heart of the Rose, Inc.

a 501(c)(3) not-for-profit organization

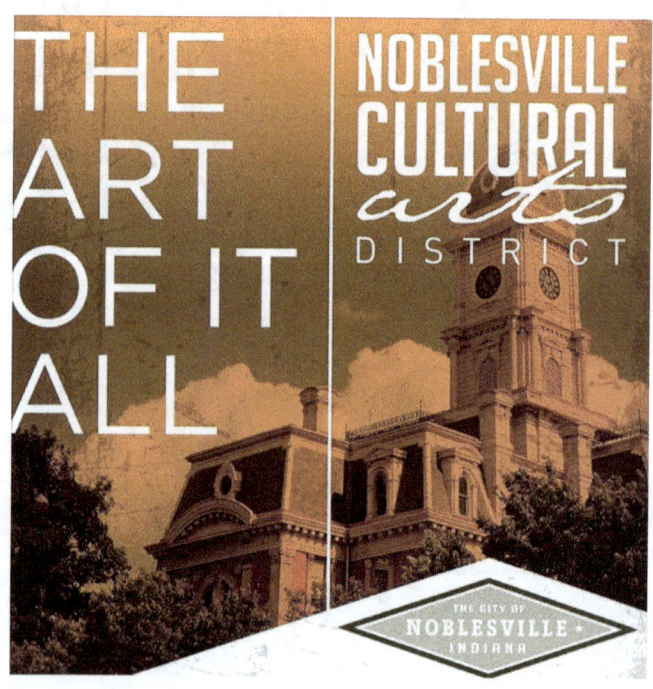

The Polk Street Review 2019 Corporate Sponsors

Logan Street Sanctuary, Inc. gratefully thanks these local businesses for their support of the 2019 edition of *The Polk Street Review*. We hope you will give them your business!

98 N. 9th Street
Downtown Noblesville

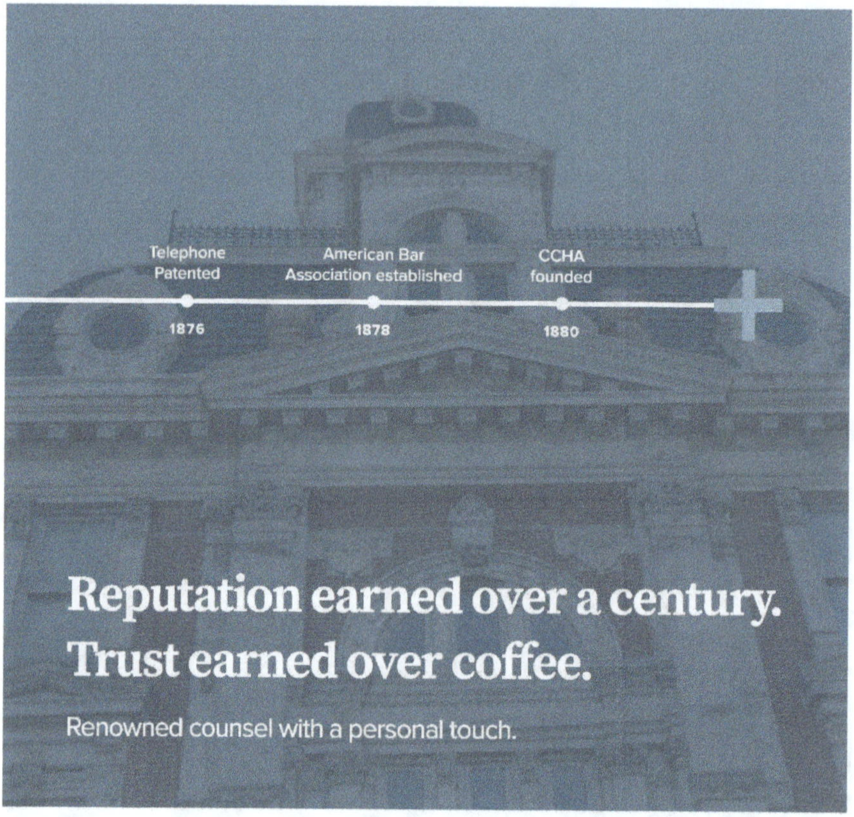

Telephone
Patented

American Bar
Association established

CCHA
founded

1876

1878

1880

Reputation earned over a century.
Trust earned over coffee.

Renowned counsel with a personal touch.

church church hittle + antrim

ATTORNEYS AT LAW

Drop by any of our offices, or give us a call. 317.773.2190

NOBLESVILLE ⋮ FISHERS ⋮ TIPTON ⋮ MERRILLVILLE ⋮ ZIONSVILLE ⋮ CCHALAW.COM

cch+a

ATTORNEYS AT LAW

Table of Contents

Introduction by Alys Caviness-Gober

Red Leaves III by Alys Caviness-Gober

As I write this introduction, it is a cold day in mid-January 2019. About 15 inches of snow fell last weekend and more is expected for the weekend ahead. I haven't really noticed the weather this month; I'm busily getting this book ready for the printer. It should be noted that, out of over 180 submissions, we have somewhere around 160 in this book. My editing partner Sarah E. and I have already gone through all the submissions, selected the ones to publish (and edited them), chosen our award winners, and I've compiled the manuscript draft into an 8.5x11 Word document. That draft went to Sarah E. for her final proofread. Keep in mind that, at this point, the submissions are simply in the draft in the order we received them, which means that multiple submissions by any one contributor are placed in the document one after another. Now, no one wants to read all five of John Doe's pieces in a row, so the submissions need to be reordered. After Sarah E.'s final proofing, I created "my" draft, which then went through at least seven permutations, as I reordered all the submissions, did a little more editing, and wrote all the stuff for the front matter and end notes. The last piece of that part of the puzzle is what I'm doing right now: writing the *Introduction*.

So yes, instead of paying attention to Old Man Winter's first and possibly last ~ fingers crossed! ~ blasts of winter weather here in Noblesville, I'm currently focused on things like Oxford commas (I *love* them) and curly quote marks, be they singles or doubles (I *hate* straight quote marks). I literally lie awake nights worrying about whether or not I caught all the straight quote marks and changed 'em to curlies, and added in all the Oxford commas that journalists and younger folk always leave out, and I spend hours every day combing through my draft, trying to catch typos and misspellings that we missed the first thousand times through (okay, okay, for Sarah E. and me combined, it was only six or seven times total) or that Word's Spellchecker won't "see" because it recognizes that things like both *and* and *an* are spelled correctly even when one or the other is contextually incorrect. Ya also gotta through in a period ever now and then, right? (*ha*, just look at my previous ten-line sentence!). Here is where I must say: *any and all remaining typos and errors are on me!*

At some point, I say, *Enough!* Because honestly, Widow & Orphan Control can just be damned, and then my real work begins ~ formatting and laying out the book to fit our 6x9 print size. That's the file that eventually becomes this book.

Such are my January days and nights every year since *Logan Street Sanctuary, Inc.* (LSS) started publishing *The Polk Street Review* three years ago. Yes, friends, the 2019 edition of *The Polk Street Review* is the third one we've published! LSS took on publishing from *The Polk Street Review*'s "founding fathers" and local authors Bill Kenley and Kurt Meyer in 2016 with the publication of the 2017 edition. As always, I'm grateful to Bill and Kurt for creating such a book in the first place, and for allowing LSS to continue to produce it. Special personal shout out to Bill, who continues to be a great supporter of the book. I'm so happy he sent in another one of his great stories this year. By the way, Bill, I enjoy reading your stories about running *far more* than I ever enjoyed *actually* running!

Now, friends, *The Polk Street Review* is special. It celebrates a place called Noblesville. It celebrates Noblesville's people and businesses ~ past and present ~ in words and images, with original songs and poems and memoirs and fiction and photographs and artwork. Everything in the book connects to Noblesville. In fact, that fact remains the one rule for submissions: all contributors *or* their subject matter must connect to Noblesville.

This year's book is chock-full of wonderful stuff celebrating Noblesville. The 2019 theme brought in some amazing pieces: poignant, hilarious, sobering, thought-provoking ~ we have it all, as people looked back, reflected on the past, imagined the future, evaluated lessons learned, or just plain told a good story through word or image. We're happy that our *International Connection Section*, sponsored by Love's Hangover Creations, includes some wonderful images and writings representing contributors' international experiences. At least three of our award-winning submissions this year can be found in the International Connection Section of the book.

A little about the awards (you'll find list near the end of the book). Let me tell you, selecting award winners is a tough job, and this year was no exception. I truly believe that every single piece of writing and images in this book deserves to be recognized as exceptional, but *1)* no one closely related to anyone on the LSS Board is eligible for awards (Board Officers are listed in the end notes), and *2)* with 160-odd published pieces, we can't give out that many awards!

The awards for each of our three submission categories (*Prose, Song Lyrics & Poetry*, and *Images*) are: *First Place, Second Place, Third Place*, and three *Honorable Mentions*. Images submitted to go along with a written piece are not eligible for *Image Category* awards. We have three *Special Awards* this year: *Special Awards* are given in recognition of something that's kind of hard to put into words, but I'll try. *Special Awards* recognize not one particular piece of writing or imagery, but rather a contributor. No matter how many pieces he or she submitted, a *Special Award* goes to a contributor that represents an element of what this book strives to do: include as many diverse styles, voices, perspectives, and elements of Noblesville as possible! We look for work that shows us the contributor is taking a risk (in life or art form), has a fresh (often younger!) perspective or voice, or has submitted something that is somehow quite different than most of the submissions we receive. It's exciting to have three *Special Award* winners this year!

The Polk Street Review's highest honor, and the final award given out at the *Awards Presentations* at our annual book launch, is the *Award of Merit*, which we've nicknamed *Best in Book*. The *Award of Merit* recognizes one submission in any of the three categories that hits our *trifecta*: it is technically and artistically outstanding, meets our theme, and elicits an emotionally connective reaction. The *Award of Merit* piece is one that is felt deeply, in your heart and soul, for a long time.

Selecting the *Award of Merit* winner, and all the other awards winners, is not an easy part of our publishing process. We hope you'll appreciate our awards selections this year. On a personal note, I hope you enjoy reading the entire book as much as I enjoyed putting it together!

~ *Alys Caviness-Gober*

(written sometime in mid-January 2019)

Noblesville Alumni on the Shore by Danika Geisler
(*Lake Powell, Utah*)

The Namesake by Nancy Simmonds

To Lavinia Noble from Josiah Polk

Lavinia, small and serene
dark eyes deep like the depths of this White River.
Watchful.

Oh Lavinia, brown hair curled
to catch the light
like the spring leaves in these tall trees.

Lavinia in the yellow dress
like daffodils in the April air.
Trembling.

Her hand in mine
as she says yes.

Lavinia, my love,
may this plot of land
endure
as a testament to my abiding love for you.

Oh Lavinia,
forever more than just my own.

Out, Out, Brief Candle! by Maik Strosahl

The strike
Of a match,

The wail of
First breath
Ignited
And wicked away
To wax,
To wain

As time flows
Over the side,
Puddling back –
Borrowed from
And returning
To earth,
Too soon.

Was that not
Just yesterday?
Did this taper
Pass in
But a moment,
As it leans
Like Pisa's tower,
As the blackened wick
Droops to
Arthritic knees
In prayer
For forgiveness,
For acceptance
Back to the dirt
That birthed it?

And just that fast,
It is extinguished.
Only the wisp
Of its smoke remains
One instant longer
Until the wind blows
To take it away
With yesterday's dust.

Four Metaphors by Celeste Williams

One: I Am

I am a writer.
A dealer in metaphor.

There is nothing which exists, ever,
that cannot be compared
to something else.

Everything reminds us
of every thing.

The allusions are illusions, really.

Yet, the best metaphors evoke
a feeling of recognition –
Like she gets when she
sees someone
she has met before.

Out of context,
the person
seems strange
and out of place.

But the dawning recognition –
… A-ha!
Places order again
where there was none.

Two: I Wrote

I wrote a play
About Frederick Douglass.

Then I was diagnosed
with cancer. In my left breast.

I wanted the Civil War
in my play

to be fought;
the South vanquished;

Douglass freed;
and his laments

about "the fraud
of Reconstruction"

to be replaced
by hope for

"More light;"
and applause…

before my surgeon
wielded his scalpel.

Three: I Would Fight

I would fight my own Civil War –
Vanquish the cancer
which had attacked my corpus –
then, face my own Reconstruction
full of hope?

I read Audre Lorde's Cancer Journal
after my surgery.

Sister Audre would agree,
metaphorically,
with Brother Douglass,
who called Reconstruction
"a stupendous fraud."
For Sister Audre called reconstruction
after mastectomy
a "cosmetic sham."

Douglass, also a purveyor
of metaphor,
called slavery a living scourge:
"The deadly [tree],
root and branch,
leaf and fibre,
body and sap,
must be utterly destroyed," he wrote.

Well, my enemy
has been vanquished
My Reconstruction,
a success.

Four: I Find Myself

I find myself
wishing Racism
could be removed
like my cancer –

Vanquished to a
compost pile
where
historical waste

decomposes
into soil,
where worms
eat

and shit
to nurture
flowers
and

peace.

Rising Above by Leslie Ober

Belles Lettres by Deborah Petersen
(a 2018 *NICE* entry, inspired by *The Odyssey*)

(*A Letter on Being Savvy* – inspired by Penelope in Homer's *The Odyssey)*

My Darlings:

I do hope this correspondence is finding you well and happy. I thought I would reach out to share some thoughts as I drink this tea and watch the leaves turn colors outside the kitchen window.

I have had the pleasure of re-visiting and enjoying the story of Penelope, Odysseus's wife, and still I am amazed at her cunning. So, here is this woman warrior, of sorts, who fended off tribes of suitors for years without shield or sword. She is a Warrior of Wit, of Savvy. One of my favorite characters!

So, how can one emulate her savvy? What can we call upon to keep us strong? How do we "unravel" (as she had done) those unwanted situations in our lives?

Here is what I have learned:

First: Pay Attention. There is a Hindu word: "*chitta*" that means just this. I define it as "a Poet's Awareness." By paying attention, you begin to hear the words unspoken, you tap into the stories untold, you are able to touch into the soul of the situation, for your focus guides you to its source.

Second: Others cross your Path daily – at work, at the store, at the gym, at the coffeehouse. They cross your Path and you cross theirs. Look at this as a Holy Communion. Be detached, without judgement. Be empathetic and radiate a compassion. What does he bring to me? What do I have to offer her?

Lastly: Praise your gifts for you have Penelope's wit and savvy. You have all that it takes to fend off the monsters. Paying attention, empathy and compassion, and this wit and savvy will be the shield and sword you have at hand always.

I believe in you.

All my love.

(*Letter on Strength* – inspired by Mary Draper Engels' *Follow the River* by James Alexander Thom)

My Darlings:

My recent readings have included a wonderful story about a woman of strength, of perseverance, of endurance. It is a story that includes deep, dark depths, a journey, a longing, a sadness, a renewal.

It brings me to this place, to this pen, to talk with you for just a brief moment.

You, too, have a strength, an inner strength, a mental and spiritual strength, encoded in your genes. A strength in our DNA from our maternal heritage. Our womenfolk may not have been hostage to a cruel tribe, but they had been hostages to a wild frontier, some, to relationships that left them in bruises, to child bearing that took its worst toll, to the diseases that also ride in the DNA alongside this strength.

I have seen this strength in you in these first few decades of your life and I am pleased, so pleased that you are gifted with this feminine blessing, a gift to you from your mother's mother and on and on.

I know there will be days when you can only feel weakness, days of aimlessness, nakedness, of debilitating sadness. There will be emotions and events and sharp words and pain and hopelessness. But it will be your strength, your birthright, that will allow you and lead you to embrace the confusion. These 'sins' fuel that fire.

Sometimes, all it takes is a walk in the woods.

Become the crunch of your feet in the ground; become the rhythm of the air dancing with your inhalations and exhalations; see passed the greens and browns and shadows and sun rays to the no-time of the woods' existence. Let the woods, this moment feed you and hold you and include you in its web for you are it and it is you.

Which leads me to this thought from another author (Palmer Parker, FB/Internet):

"Self-care is never a selfish act – it is simply good stewardship of the only gift I have! The gift I was put on earth to offer to others. Any time we can listen to True Self, and give it the care it requires, we do so not only for ourselves, but for the many others whose lives we touch."

But, that, my Dears, is for another letter, another cup of tea.

All my love.

River Dreams by Alys Caviness-Gober

Cadence 23 by Jim Caviness

(*Editor's Note*: a *military cadence* is a call-and-response song sung by military personnel while running or marching.)

Running in the desert at 110,
If you think that's it, best think again.
Operation Northern Edge in the ice and snow,
If you think of that, then you don't know.
Hell week and he didn't ring the bell,
That's closer now, but I'm here to tell
I've been side by side with ranger and seal,
Salty, yeah, but not the real deal.
37 hours she broke her own tail bone,
No medication she was all alone.
Or holding that baby we couldn't save,
Rocking gently as she turned cold and grey.
She turns and pulled her son to her chest,
Grief and pain, but never time to rest
Sound off, feel tough; but know what's tougher:
Nothing in this world will ever top a mother.

Anchors Away by Danika Geisler
(*Lake Powell, Utah*)

Never (still too soon) by John Gilmore
(*song lyric*)

You ain't real sharp said the knife to the spoon
You might as well throw rocks at the man in the moon
You're just wasting your time
That's all you're doin'

You can beat a dead horse but it still won't run
There's been too much said and too much done
between the two of us
that can't be undone

So I'm just sittin' on my porch whistlin' a tune
and thinking if I never see you again

it'll be too soon
Never's still too soon

You got your shades of gray and your shades of blue
I'd have turned and run away from you
the very day we met
if I'd only knew

Ah, but that was then and this is now
of course I can't go back but if I could somehow
ya know I'd burn that bridge
before I crossed it

Because I tried too hard for way too long
You never tried at all unless I'm wrong
but I'm afraid I'm right
I really wish I was wrong

I've got troubles I've borrowed and troubles I've bought
and a lot of bad thoughts I wish I'd never have thought
and you were one tough lesson
I wish I'd never been taught

Well I'm not that dumb and I'm not blind
but this out of sight and out of mind
well it ain't that easy
at least it's not for me

So I'm just sittin' on my porch and whistlin' this tune
thinkin' if I never see you again
it'll be too soon
Never's still too soon

Better Days by Vivian Belle

If I'd have known
way back then
that Better Days
would come,

I'd have

worried less

> about how I looked
> what "*they*" thought

smiled more

> at boys
> at my parents
> at strangers

partied harder

> like, *WAY* harder!

laughed out loud a lot (*lolal*?)

> a lot more

I'd have rolled

No

I'd have rock'n'rolled
with life's punches
with a lot more aplomb.

Ruby Boots (aka, What A LONG Journey) by Vivian Belle

What I Could Have Been by Leslie Ober

I could have been a prima ballerina . . . a dancer extraordinaire, but my five-year-old self was not into it as many of the little girls were. I have no memories of even being in ballet class, so this part of my story is told from my mother's perspective.

It was the big day – the day that all of the parents got to join the ballet class to see what their precious daughters had been up to for the past few weeks.

It was a time for these twirling tutus to get to show off their new skills.

All of the girls lined up to the bar and began their pliés in beautiful unison, with the exception of one red-headed child, who stood with one hand on the bar and the other hand busily picking her nose. This child was completely unaware of anything going on around her. She was off in some kind of day dream world, completely oblivious of the attention that she was drawing to herself as she snacked away on her nasal findings.

My mother was mortified. She sunk in her seat, hoping no one would realize that it was HER daughter that was enjoying a mid-dance-class snack in front of everyone. She thought she had raised me better. As the story goes, once she got me into the car and out of sight of anyone in class, she scolded me.

In her exasperation, she implored, "Do you want to do ballet or would you rather pick your nose?"

And from the backseat, I confidently shouted, "*I WANT TO PICK MY NOSE!*"

I never took another ballet class so long as I have lived. And if there were a professional sport at nose picking, I would have surely succeeded there!

Little Ballerinas by Leslie Ober

Life Lost in Living by Mary Couch

If I had known, how my life would turn out.
Perhaps, I would have sought a different path,
danced in the rain, walked with you on the shore,
played with the kids, not worked late each night.

Had I known then, our life would be so short,
I would have spent more time there by your side,
race barefoot with you through velvet grass
beneath moonlight nights to swim in the lake.

I would not have worried what others thought,
wore plaid with polka dots or even stripes,
danced in grocery aisles, played Pied Piper
while the kids followed me around the block.

I would have done somersaults in the yard,
caught snowflakes on my tongue,
took that vacation you always wanted,
not worked double shifts, or long weekends.

Instead, I watched my life from a distance,
a shadow figure who did not exist.
Had I only known my future, perhaps;
I would not have lost my life in living.

Father's Day 2018 by Alys Caviness-Gober

June 17th. Father's Day. I miss my dad. Four years ago today, he had
the stroke that killed him (after a week on life support). I've written
about that day before. I wish its four-year anniversary hadn't fallen on
Father's Day this year, my first Father's Day without my mom, who
passed away July 8th, 2017.

Bittersweet now is June for me. June 17th now marks the beginning
of what was a week of Hell in 2014; Dad died on June 23rd, three
days after my birthday. This year is my first birthday month (June)
without my mom. The loss of Mom has sharpened the loss of Dad.

This year, I'll have my first birthday without both my parents. *I wish I wish I wish* a lot of things about my folks, but mostly I just wish I could hug them both once more.

Photos are priceless, and I treasure the ones I have that Mom took on holidays and birthdays, of Dad and us kids together, and I treasure the ones I took later of my folks with my kids on holidays and birthdays. But I don't have a lot of photos of just me and my dad or just my dad alone that are not a holiday or birthday. I don't have any photos of my real memories. I don't have any photos of me with my dad, working on projects around the house (in our house in Georgia, or here, in the magic house I live in now), working in the yard (Georgia or here), fishing or kayaking (mostly Georgia, but a little bit here), running together (Georgia and here). I don't have video or recordings of our conversations as I biked behind him as he ran 18-20 miles on the (now overdeveloped) back roads of our little corner of Hamilton County.

Yesterday, I was in a workshop writing a memoir for this book; there's a bit about my dad in it, maybe not my best memory of a moment with him, but certainly one that shaped my life. So much of my dad shaped my life. I wish I had a photo of every great memory I have of Dad ~ but, I don't. I wasn't raised in a time when random minutes of life or "doing" mundane things in a photo was instantly immortalized like with today's quick cell phone snaps.

My advice to people my kids' age who might get annoyed by us older folks wanting to snap those cell phone shots and little videos of every little thing you do together every time we older folks see you: *LET US*. Let us have photos and little videos of *YOU* with us. Let us capture our memories of time with you as often as possible.

I have memories. I wish I could touch them like a photograph. I wish I could walk in a room and see my dad sitting in his chair, with that look on his face; expectant, waiting for me to talk to him about my kids or art or movies. *I wish I wish I wish* a lot of things about my dad, but mostly I just wish I could hug him once more and say, *Happy Father's Day, Dad, I love you.*

Collision by Jansen Sovich
(a 2018 *NICE* entry, inspired *The Three Musketeers*)

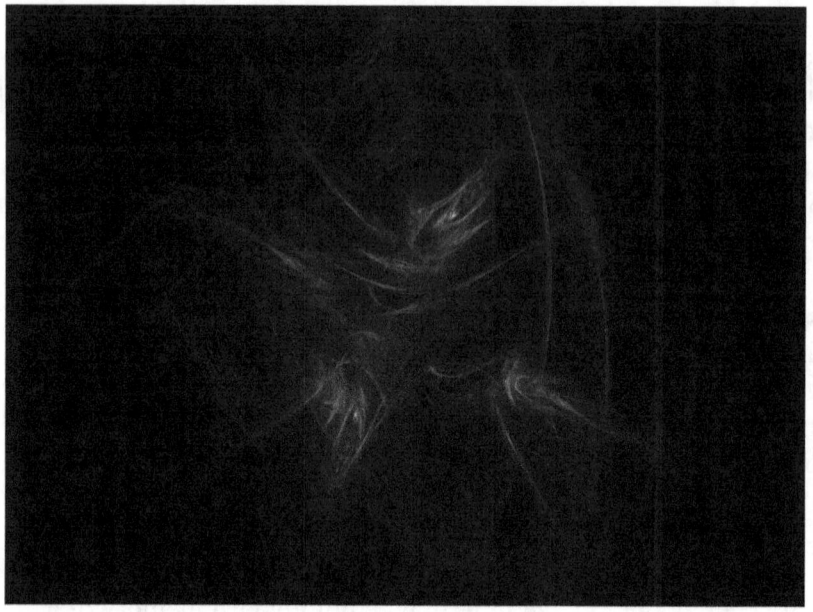

Miss Betty Boop Has Now Retired by Jenny Kalahar

She held out hope
Until her heart grew weary in waiting for a comeback that did not
come
Miss Boop dismissed her agent and publicist at last –
Those who had all but dismissed her long years ago

With her purse full of savings that had been earned at the hands of
animators
On the wavelengths of voice artists
And by the words of unseen cartoon writers
    all of whom had thought they knew her best
She left that fading California life by train and headed east

Miss Boop had said her goodbyes with her own lilting voice –
A tender alto so much richer than her borrowed baby soprano
She gave away her hair clips and tiny black dresses
Her tiny high heels and hula skirts

And moved to small-town, sunflower-shaded Indiana
　　to a house that felt like home at last

Calling herself Bettina Blossom
She spends her days gardening, loving the zooming bees and writhing
worms
Letting her pale, soft knees grow calloused in the moist dirt
She snaps photos of squirrels and cardinals in the neighborhood park
at dawn
And takes cooking lessons on Friday evenings, no longer afraid of
steam

Miss Blossom is finding happiness
Not with her practiced innocent sexuality
Not with her old "dontchawanta kiss me" big-eyed ways
Bettina is a creature transformed –
　　now no longer dependent upon the attention of men to survive

She is fond of letting her slim fingers dawdle over the bluesy lower
keys
　　on her back-porch, out-of-tune piano
In the morning she raises her hands to run those fingers through her
graying hair
Gray now that her inky dye bottle has been placed far back in a
drawer
Without a single eraser on her makeup table
Her forehead is growing lined, her jowls are drooping
As she has become both tougher and softer as the months float by

Miss Blossom composes her own dialogue now
She does not have to mouth words spoken by voice artists
And though she stumbles over uncertain declarations
It's all fine; it's all so sweet and unrehearsed
And her tongue is learning to flow, easy and smooth
　　with her own, honest feelings

She sometimes misses the old days, and fame
Glorious fame, when she wanted to be loved by you
　　just you and nobody else but you
But that feeling passes in a soft flip, like a turned page

Now she is invited to Tupperware parties and bookclub meetings
She watches old silent movies on Saturdays with the ladies up the
street
And grocery-shops on Sundays with her good friend, Mavis
Bettina builds little newsprint and comic-strip houses
For the girls next door who call her "Grandma"
    and who hold her hands and laugh

No one here knows about her past
It's as if she's always lived in Indiana, always waved and gardened,
always *was*
But one day a young reporter came knocking after searching many
leads
Excited, he begged for an interview, for a photo, for some proof
But she had to state, in all truthfulness, that Betty Boop does not live
in Indiana
He had the wrong house
She is just a tiny old lady with honorary grandchildren
Who weeds and cooks and reads
A small-town, independent soul who enjoys speaking her own,
heartfelt words
And with that the reporter stood, smiled, and kissed her paper-thin
cheek
He had to agree

He left her standing gracefully in her overflowing garden
    another velvet, fading blossom
Flecks of late-afternoon sun brushed through her straw hat
    crosshatching her tender features
And he had to agree

She had the right to disappear

Looking Back by Leslie Ober

For Rosie, my lifelong friend by Kitty O'Doherty

Thursday, June 30, 2016

My friend, my friend, my beautiful lifelong friend. How do I begin to tell you how much you've meant to me all of these years?

You have been exactly what a friend should be. You welcomed me when I was the new girl at school and from then on it was a lifetime of shared laughter, intermittent life-phase drama, and lots of fun. With you I could share any secret, any fear, any crazy dream, and you always made me feel safe. You straightened me out when I needed it, you always gave great advice, and you showed through example how not to sweat the little things in life. And you . . . you don't even sweat the very big things. You're amazing.

You've lived a great exuberant life, and I've been so lucky to have shared most of those years with you. You always seemed so brave and adventurous to me, willing to take risks in business and new paths in life. And if anything faltered, you just picked up and pointed yourself in a new direction, never even glancing behind.

To look back at us from this stage of life, I chuckle at the young, silly, boy-crazy girls we once were. Some of my most favorite memories are of all the summers between 8th grade and on through high school where we spent hours lounging by my apartment pool and flirting with boys. It was almost like a calling for us, really. You, such a tiny little thing with an hourglass figure and waist-length jet black hair, and me, just flat and tan with amateur hair bleaching skills that always kept my dark hair a dull bronze at best. Summer was our season and we kept ourselves fueled with suntan oil, vending machine Cokes, and frozen pizzas.

If we weren't at the pool, then we were most likely on our way to either your house or the apartment in which I grew up. We put a lot of miles on our feet in those days with our homes separated by a couple of parish neighborhoods. Our parents happily assimilated an additional "daughter" and our siblings all gained an additional "sister." Our home lives were so different, and you could so easily roll with the periodic craziness that was mine. I loved your big family, and the controlled loving chaos of so many siblings. You had older sisters to learn from and Joe, the lone brother who was in COLLEGE, that mysterious, far-in-the-future entity. Your home and family was as welcoming and comfortable to me as falling into an oversized easy chair. Your mom was always warm and funny and ready to dispense advice – especially about boys, our favorite topic at that time! Your father was so handsome and just the kind of dad a girl should have.

Where your home was more traditional, mine was bohemian, and slightly wacky. Yours was fine furniture, soft colors, matching drapes.

Mine was black and white leather, orange vinyl, and Aretha Franklin music. I suppose when you came to my house, it was kind of a novel treat for you to experience the always colorful randomness of life there. But you were the only person I brought to my house in those days that I knew could handle what might be beyond the front door. Some days coming home from school was a lot like opening the door of a fun house. It wouldn't be unusual to walk in past the beaded curtain in my living room to see my mother, cigarette in one perfectly manicured hand, watering her houseplants in her long, lovely, leopard-print negligee set. "Hello, girls," she'd say so casually. "I baked a cheesecake, and there's fresh lemonade in the fridge. Just be sure to clean up your mess." Other times, we'd open the door and perhaps mom's artist, writer, or musician friends would be there having a jam session. We just never knew. At any of these mystery door scenes, I would sigh, and we'd both laugh, then make our way down the hall to my room. But never there was never any judgement, and no shock from you . . . you were just in the moment and taking things in stride as if this were a *normal* house.

I look back and am amused at the way we looked forward to reading our horoscopes in each month's issue of my mother's *Cosmopolitan* magazine. Cosmo's horoscope was much more fun than any others, with promises of gigantic, exciting, nearly impossible careers, and enough romance and lusty stuff to make the future look like someplace we needed to be, and fast. "Omigosh, Rosie! Your horoscope said you're going to become a financial genius and live in Tokyo with a husband you acquired in your travels to France – and that SO could happen, you are great with money, and you're part FRENCH!" Rosie, you are a true Taurus, hugely affectionate, patient, stubbornly determined, straightforward, loyal, smart and grounded, but always up for an adventure. And always in the present moment, with no regrets of the past. I, on the other hand, Libra, given to flights of fancy but on the cusp of Virgo – which means part of me has the capability to be logical, analytical, and health conscious, but the Libran side tends to override in the end. Somehow, my whimsical ways didn't drive you crazy. And you never had to bail me out of jail. But you surely would've if needed.

In a recent talk we had, you recalled one night in the summer after 8th grade when you spent the night at my place. You swear we snuck out of my bedroom window after curfew to go talk to boys. Now I'm pretty sure there's no way we would EVER have done that ;-) Would we? Okay, yes. We did.

You were Emeraude, powder blue, and soft yellow. I was Patchouli oil, purple, and hot pink. You didn't own jeans for quite some time, I was never in anything but. You were The Carpenters, I was Led Zeppelin. And yet . . . and yet we weren't so different at all. We loved going to Ritter dances. We LOVED dancing! We LOVED shopping and make-up and music and all of our school and neighborhood friends, including my neighbor, Bunny. Yes, it was a funny trio whenever we hung out – a Rose, a Kitty, and a Bunny.

We came to the end of high school and life unfolded in different ways for us. You left for college, then Michigan, then eventually California, while I stayed in Indy. You started businesses of your own and did very well. In between we had children and marriages and long distance calls to try to keep up on each nuance. (Okay, you only had one marriage, I had . . . uh, several. But you did try to talk me out of that last one, and I really should've listened!) You visited from California with your young boys (at that time my hair was accidentally a shade of maroon), and it was so sad to see you leave again. You eventually and thankfully came back to Indiana for good and surprised me by showing up at my 40th birthday party. It was the best present ever!

Here's another thing I think about when I think of you. We've both have always been animal lovers. However, my pets have always run around naked. YOU dressed your cat and dog in Colts outfits on game day Sundays. I told you I couldn't believe I had a friend who did that kind of thing. But you insisted that they loved it. And you know, they probably did.

The Facebook pictures of us from 2011 taken at the lake? Yes, there you are bouncing in the water on your floaty and when I slowly slinked myself from the dock into the water you called out to tell me to be careful, you'd seen a nest of baby snakes in the water RIGHT THERE. But hey, you calmly assured me they were harmless. Nevertheless, I know I must've impressed you with my sudden ability to walk on water.

You had a strong faith, and a real knack for living one day at a time. Truly living each day to the fullest. Your family, from your sons, your siblings, your, what now, about 762 nieces and nephews, have always been the most important people in your life. I'm sorry, DesRoches family, but I lost count pretty much after Lisa, Kim, Denise, Paul, Josh, Kevin, Michelle, Melanie, and Marie were born. Every family photo you guys post has a new member, whether the addition is through a newly married niece or nephew or a brand new baby. Rosie, I know you simply cherished each new addition to this wonderful, wonderful family and you were always thrilled to share each new announcement.

You cried when you told me you were sick. You rarely cried in all of our life. But you didn't cry out of fear for yourself, you cried because you knew I was handling a family illness and you didn't want to add to my worries. Last week, when you told me you were going to be under hospice care, you stopped me short and told me not to worry, then pointed out all of the positives – of which you named many. You simply have never wanted anyone to worry about you.

Our approach to life couldn't have been more different at times. Where I was fast and impulsive, you were thoughtful and took your time. Where I was slow and fearful, you plunged whole heartedly. I think we truly learned from each other, I know I learned much from you. And I am still learning. I'm learning that it's okay to continue to laugh. Even through tears. I don't like this kind of laughing with you. It's not what I expected, it's not what I want for you or your sons or your entire family. This is not how it's supposed to be. I expected your laugh to ring on forever and ever, with no end. No tears and no end. But dear Rosie, please know that no matter what, in my heart and my head, I will always, always, always hear your laugh, your giggle, your voice.

Always with love, my dear friend.

Kitty

(Started as a letter to Rosie on June 30th, 2016 . . . ended up being her eulogy, July 8th, 2016)

Two Bottom Bob by Michael Stewart
(*song lyric*)

This fellow named Bob had forty acres
That needed plowed but he got no takers
All his nearby farming friends and neighbors said no
"This part of the season I don't have time
If I was going to be plowing I'd be plowing mine
Sorry Bob but the answer's no"
But Bob had a little plow that he used in his garden
So he took it down there and he knew it'd be a hard one
But the task at hand needed doing just the same
He hooked the plow up and it turned just fine
So he plowed that field two rows at a time
And that's how he got the name Two Bottom Bob

He plowed that forty acres with a two bottom plow
Took him nigh forever but he got it done somehow
Sheer determination, he didn't whine or sob
There ain't no job too big for Two Bottom Bob

Well after it was plowed it was going to need disking
And he knew his farming friends weren't risking
Their big old rigs in that tiny plot
But one had an old disk rusting in a field
And after they had wheeled and dealed
Bob paid for just what he got
It would make one pass before it'd break down
So he'd put it back together and turn around
Then do the same thing on the other side
After days and days of busting clods
He got the job done against all odds
An accomplishment in which he took great pride

He plowed that forty acres with a two bottom plow
Took him nigh forever but he got it done somehow
Sheer determination, he didn't whine or sob
There ain't no job too big for Two Bottom Bob

Well the co-op boys had seen Bob in the field
And they inquired of his intended yield
Bob said "It's a pollinator crop,
Pretty little flowers, beneficial plants
Sustenance for birds to ants"
As he explained all their jaws dropped
They said "Two Bottom that was a plowing feat
But after all that work you got nothing to eat
You're growing food for butterflies and bees"
Bob said "I made the world a more beautiful place
I filled that field with joy and grace
And I'm collecting wicked subsidies

He plowed that forty acres with a two bottom plow
Took him nigh forever but he got it done somehow
Sheer determination, he didn't whine or sob
There ain't no job too big for Two Bottom Bob

Frayed Jeans, Flannel Shirts by Sam Watermeier

MTV Music Awards,
1992.
Nirvana plays "Lithium,"
an opiate for the audience.
Frayed jeans, flannel shirts,
flailing angst, overcast skies.
One with the Seattle sun.
Kurt Cobain's chords rumble,
like rolling thunder.
"I like it,
I'm not gonna crack,"
he belts.
But that's what grunge is
– cracking,
a seismic shift,
imperfection as beauty,
music that says,
"I'm so ugly,
but that's OK

’cause so are you.”
Stringy hair, sooty shirts,
raw nerves ripped like jeans.
Grunge brings out the lepers,
lets them drain their wounds,
makes them say,
“Here we are now,
entertain us.”

Grieving for Grunge Gods by Sam Watermeier

If I Only Knew by David Allen

What would life be like
if I could somehow sail
back to the earlier me
and let that youngster avail
himself to all that I know now?

Musing on this,
munching on the memories
of the path that delivered me
to this cluttered, book-filled room
it didn't take me long at all
to turn the idea down.

I'm not sure I'd want to be
the person who,
avoiding the pitfalls
and taking advantage
of the successes,
became someone else.

Pissing Contests by Bill Kenley

"You know Kindle, I really don't like to race you," Wally Hawkard
said. We were jogging together on the edge of the Ridgeline football
and track stadium parking lot. It was a warm, humid spring night.
Huge banks of blue-white stadium lights floated like UFOs in the near
distance. The announcer's voice, monotonous and official, echoed out
into the surrounding darkness. *Second call, girls 800 meter run.
Second call...*

I remember how cool I thought it was. Wally and me, a Ridgeline
Saluki and a Pennsgap Snapper, a freshman and a senior, natural
enemies on two counts, warming up for the 3200 meter run at our
Conference track meet together. Then Wally ruined it.

"Wally, a race is not some kind of pissing contest," I said as we
shuffled together off of the parking lot and onto a quiet, dark, tree-
lined street. Then, although I knew the answer, I asked the question he
was begging for. "Okay... Why don't you like to race me?"

"I don't like to race you because I don't *hate* you," he said. "I like to
hate my opponent. You're such a nice guy. It's confusing." He glared
hard at me as we jogged as if he wanted me to apologize for being a
nice guy. I obliged, as nice guys will.

"I'm sorry I'm nice and you find it hard to hate me," I said.

"Don't do that!" he said. "How am I ever gonna hate you if you apologize when I try to hate you?"

Wally's aggressive nature manifested itself in several aspects his appearance. He had a fierce buzz cut so high and tight it was nearly a Mohawk. I could easily imagine him as a Lakota warrior at Little Big Horn in a pair of buckskins, shirtless and covered in war paint, a bloody knife in one hand and the ragged, red-dripping scalp of one of General George Armstrong Custer's cavalrymen raised up in the other or as a gung-ho Marine at Khe Sahn, charging up some muddy hill with an M16, his beady eyes bouncing around, looking to zap Charlie Cong.
In addition to his warrior haircut, his eyebrows were almost perpetually slanted inward toward the bridge of his nose and the skin there between his eyes was crinkled together. It was like he perpetually smelled something disagreeable.

"Damn you, Sherman," he said, the crease in between his eyes in heavy relief in the dim yellow light of a streetlamp, "you're just not a very good enemy."

"No offense, but you're a damaged individual, Wally."

"Fuck you, Sherman," he replied.

We slowed to a walk, kicking our legs and shaking out our arms. "Okay. Fuck me," I said, a smile on my face. "Feel better? You hate me now?"

"No," he replied with a disappointed sigh. "There's no hope. You're too nice. Let's just stretch."
While I didn't agree with Wally's approach to competition, I see now that he wasn't an unusual athlete. I was the weird one.

It starts sometime after the childhood days of mercy rules and post-game Capri Suns and Oreos are over and coaches start looking to stir the fire in the bellies of their young athletes by cultivating in them an attitude of loathing and disgust toward opposing teams and athletes.

They begin to sell the idea that those other guys in the other jerseys are trying to take what is rightfully theirs. They insinuate disrespect on the grounds of difference. So, lots of athletes learn to hate their opponents. Of course, some athletes don't need a coach's instructions – they hate their opponents all by themselves, no teaching necessary. Either way, Wally *was* unusual in the scorching hatred he manufactured for his opposition for a runner.

While we runners may not love our competitors, in most of us the suffering at the heart of every distance race pares away the illusion of otherness. By the time we're done, hands on hips, gulping air, leaning into each other just to stay upright, runners generally feel nothing but respect for those willing to suffer as much as they do. We're all the same in the chute as we crumble into ourselves after we've given the last measure of all we've got, defeated by something much larger than another human being. Wally apparently never felt that transcendent union most of us welcome at the end of a race. He wouldn't allow it. For him, victory was the only reason to run, and victory was entirely and completely about beating others. Hatred, he seemed to believe, was an effective tool when it came to achieving victory.

Months before, that Fall at a cross-country meet in the countdown to race time, I'd happened upon a scene that gave me my first insight into Wally's particular and peculiar runner's mind. He was taking a pee at a urinal when a kid from Jasper High School stepped up to the urinal next to him.

"Ridgeline Salukis?" the kid said quietly, reading from the back of Hawkard's t-shirt. The kid put a question mark on it like the two words together were some strange novelty, as if Ridgeline were some no-name squad he'd never heard of before. This was a bit ridiculous as they'd won a dozen state titles in a row.
"Yeah," said Wally without looking up, annoyed by the kid's silly gamesmanship. "That's right," he said, the edge of a growl in his voice. "Ridgeline Salukis."

"What exactly is a Saluki?" the kid asked as he settled in and began tinkling away.

Wally didn't respond, but I could tell he was steamed. It was the sound of his pee hitting the ceramic surface of the urinal that clued me in. It was a furious splattering. Wally was literally pissed off. I half expected him to turn his hot stream on the right leg of Jasper runner standing next to him.

"Well, good luck today," the kid said pleasantly, overlooking Wally's dismissal of his question.

From behind the two of them I let escape a short bark of a laugh before I could contain myself. I knew what Hawkard was thinking.

Hawkard was thinking that the kid was trying to get into his head. Trying put his team on the same level as Ridgeline, state champs every year in a row since before he was old enough to talk. He was thinking that the kid was suggesting that maybe it was only luck that would determine which team ended up winning and which team ended up losing on this particular day. *Good luck!* Hawkard was thinking. *What a laugh!* Luck had nothing to do with anything.

Deep down in his fiery soul, he was loving it. It was what he needed to take him over the top just before go time. I prepared myself to enjoy whatever happened next. Wally didn't let me down.

"Well, bad luck to you," Hawkard growled as he pulled up his shorts and slapped the toilet flusher. He turned his bright blue eyes on the kid. "And Ridgeline doesn't need it. Any kind of luck."

He leaned toward him and poked him in the shoulder with his finger. "We're the Ridgeline Salukis you dickweed nobody. You'll remember that after today. I'm gonna kick your ass." When he turned away from the kid and saw me standing there waiting by the door for a john, a smile on my face, Wally turned his rage on me. "Laugh it up, Kindle. You pathetic Turtle . . . I'm gonna kick your ass too."

"Okay, Wally. Okay," I said as he brushed past me.

He kicked the door open.

"Hey!" I said.

Wally turned and stared at me.

"Good luck today, Wally."

Of course, he went on to run a personal record.

But that night before the Conference two-mile, I'd had enough of Hawkard's attitude.

"You want to hate me?" I said. "That's a stupid freshman thing to say. You *want* to *hate* me?"

The weariness of being a senior washed over me in that moment. I felt a psychic twinge at the thought of our race about a half-hour into the future. I thought of those sixth and seventh laps, always tough, then the gun going into that last quarter. I thought of Wally Hawkard on my shoulder, frothing at the mouth, breathing down my neck the whole time, his brain churning and fuming like some engine fueled by a toxic blend of suspicion and disgust. God . . . Why did I put myself through it?

"It's not a stupid freshman thing to say," replied Hawkard. "You're just too nice. I wish you were a dick."

"Be careful what you wish for," I said.

We quit stretching and began our jog back toward the track, the stadium lights glowing and buzzing overhead. I attempted to be the wise mentor to Hawkard – to be his Yoda before hate consumed him and he went total Darth Vader, never to return from the Dark Side.

"Wally, I want to run *with* people, not *against* them. I want to run against myself. I want to run as fast as I can, and I want you to help me do that by running with me. You know? Pushing each other to greatness. That kind of thing."

Hawkard shook his head and the skin between his eyes did its angry nose crinkle thing. "I don't get it," he said. "That doesn't make sense. The only point of racing is beating you. You and everyone else in the race."

I sighed in response. Words had failed me.

That two-mile run at Conference was the last time I ever ran with or against Wally, a fact that didn't create wistful nostalgia in me. When I crossed the line that night, I was happy to be done with Hawkard. I finished about ten meters behind him – fourth to his third. We'd been neck and neck with a hundred to go. Wally had kicked and left me in the final straight. He'd found another gear when I couldn't, tapping into an energy source I seemed to lack.

Three years passed and one late spring day I returned from college and moved back into my old room. It took about two hours for the doldrums of life-not-at-college to set in, and, out of boredom, I picked up a Tupperware container with all my ribbons from all my high school races. I began sifting through them and they turned into memories.

Everyone remembers blue for first, red for second, and white for third. And I remembered those races, especially the rare blues. But as I picked through my ribbons, I was amazed at how clear my memories were, even the races I would've thought I'd have forgotten.

Here was a yellow for fourth at the Bronco Invitational. That had been a dark, sloppy day. I remembered a wash of brown on my lower legs as I sat in the wet, bright green grass after the race, my shorts soaked to the point of dripping. Clots of dirt hung from the hair on my shins. Leo Chavez's face, his black hair wet and plastered to his skull, hovered above me.

"Dude, you got a bad case of the shingleberries."

I just looked up at him, exhausted and confused. The glaring gray sky made my head feel like it was full of helium.
"You know…" Leo said, his hand out to me to pull me off the ground. "Like dingleberries but hanging onto your shinhairs, not your butthairs."

Here was a pink for sixth in the 800 at the Hamilton County Meet my junior year–a night Coach tried to double me in the 400 and 800. The rest had been too short after my hard effort in the quarter. The invisible chimp that climbed on near the six-hundred-meter mark had never been larger. I remembered the feeling of being drawn backwards somehow. It didn't feel like a monkey on my back that day, more like a six-hundred-pound silverback gorilla.

A brown ribbon. Cross Country Regionals my senior year. Hawkard stood next to me. "Look at that, Wally," I said with a smile. "Brown." We were stretched out in line at the awards ceremony. I held up my eighth-place ribbon for him to inspect. A beautiful clear autumn evening was coming on fast, the air crisp and cold, darkness descending. "Like a turd."

"Better than gray," he said from my left. He'd come in one spot behind me. A man in a tan jacket snapped pictures of us for the newspaper. His flash popped.

"I'd rather have gray than this flat turd." I turned the ribbon over in my hand. The gold imprinting was hard to read. "This thing is just ugly."

Hawkard had snatched the ribbon out of my hand then and pushed his gray one into mine. Then, when he realized I was going to accept the trade, that I didn't really care if he kept my eighth-place ribbon, he snatched his gray ninth-place ribbon back and shoved mine into the pocket of my warm-up jacket, acting as if I'd been trying to dupe him into trading all along.

I put the ribbons back in the little translucent box and set it back on my shelf to be forgotten again.

"You ought to go to the Conference Track Meet tonight," my dad said at dinner that night.

I shrugged. "That's ancient history," I said. I hadn't run a race on a track in three years. I hadn't really run much at all in that time to speak of. A few late-night stress relievers to break up study sessions was about it.

"There's a freshman you ought to see," he said. "He's the best distance runner Pennsgap's ever had."

"Better than Uncle Jack?" I asked.

Dad's eyebrows arched. He smiled. "That's who told me he's the best distance runner Pennsgap's ever had."

My uncle, it turned out, was right.

At fourteen years old, Noel Starks stood five-eleven. I know it's not physically possible, but four of those nearly six feet of height seemed made up of a pair of thin, muscular legs. The kid's calves were like river stones, hard and flat, the outer stones slightly smaller and higher on his leg then the inner ones. They were Kenyan calves if I've ever seen them on a white boy.

He had a keg-shaped upper body just big enough to fit in a pair of huge and super-efficient lungs. From that oxygen-delivery system hung a pair of long, spindly arms. There was something arachnid about him. He just needed four more of those long limbs and six of those crazy, black, soulless spider eyes and he'd have been good for a web. I later learned he didn't just look like a spider, he was as heartless and as predatory as one as well. Worse, actually. I've never heard of spiders playing with their prey.

By the time I got there, just before the two mile run, Starks had already won the mile and the eight-hundred. Good times, great times for a freshman – 4:24 and 1:58, if I remember. I wasn't truly impressed, however, until the first lap of the two-mile run when he ran by, tucked in right behind Wally Hawkard who, although his face had gotten a little fuller in the years since I'd last seen him, had that same grim, angry crinkle between his eyes I remembered, the same high and tight warrior's haircut above it.

"He's tripling?" I said to the group of Snapper distance guys I was leaning against the chain link fence with, all of us looking out onto the track.

"He insisted," said a clearly smitten junior, a talentless little guy who, it was obvious, lived vicariously through Starks. "He said after he swept the distances he'd absolutely own Hawkard for the tournament."

As the laps passed, Starks stayed on Hawkard's heels, looming there behind him, biding his time until the second to last lap of the race when he moved up beside him and then, surprisingly, just stayed there.

"What's he doing?" I asked. "Running in lane two? He should take him now and break him or stay tucked in behind him and keep the heat on." Then I noticed something even odder. "Is he *talking* to him?"

"Oh yeah! He's telling him a joke," said the junior gleefully. "Every time he runs him, he tells him a joke. They all start off the same. '*A guy walks into a bar*...'"

"You're kidding me."

"Nope. He started doing it in cross country when he realized how pissed Wally, who's a senior, got when he lost to a freshman. To anyone, really. Noel's got a ton of 'A guy walks into a bar' jokes just for Wally. The one he's telling him now starts, 'A guy walks into a bar and tells the bartender he can pee in a shot glass from twenty feet away. The bartender says, 'I'll bet you a thousand bucks you can't.' The guy says, "You're on.'"

"He tells you guys the jokes? Before he races?" I asked. This seemed a bit extreme. Cockiness at its outer limits. Clearly bad karma. I wasn't sure what to think.

"Oh yeah. Every time. Before the meet starts he rehearses with us." The kid had a big smile on his face–he took pride at being a part of this ritual of ridicule. "He doesn't want to let Hawkard down by flubbing the joke or forgetting the punchline."

"Well," I said. "Tell it to me."

And as the junior told me the joke, I watched as Noel Starks' ran next to Wally Hawkard, his mouth moving. And I watched the angry crinkle in between Hawkard's eyes get deeper and deeper.

"So, the guy puts the shotglass at the end of the bar, walks back so he's across from the bartender, unzips his fly, and then he proceeds to piss all over *everything* – the bar, the bottles of booze, the bartender, *everything*."

I couldn't help but giggle a little at the image. And at the thought of Wally Hawkard being subjected to the same joke I was currently enjoying. As they made their way past the start/finish line and into the turn, the bell ringing to signify the final lap of the race, Starks kept twisting his head and talking. Wally kept staring straight ahead.

"The bartender, even though he's soaking wet with the guy's piss, roars with laughter and tells the guy to pay up. And then the guy happily pays the bartender $1000, a big grin on his face."

Hawkard and Starks were heading down the back straight.

The junior went on with the joke, "But then the bartender stops laughing, he's confused. This guy just lost $1000! Why's he – see!" the kid pointed across the track, "He just finished the joke!" And Starks bolted. Within seconds, a gap of five meters turned into ten, then fifteen, then twenty.

"Hawkard's toast," said the junior gleefully. "Just like always."

As Starks ate up the turn, Hawkard wilted behind him. He absolutely cracked. His shoulders slumped, his head dropped, and I suddenly felt bad for my old warm-up partner. "That's just sad," I said.

"Oh, you don't know all of it," said the junior. "You don't know what he says *after* the joke. Right before he leaves him in the dust."

I stared at him. He just stared back at me. "Well?" I said.

"Well what?" the kid had a confused look on his face.

"Well what does he say after the joke?"

"Oh! Well, after the punchline, he always looks at Hawkard right in the face and he says, 'Was that funny?' And Hawkard never says anything back because he's mad and knows what's going to happen next. Then, after Hawkard doesn't say anything, Starks always says,

'Well if that wasn't funny, this is.' And then he takes off and crushes Hawkard yet again."

It was just after that explanation of Starks' cruel humor that he blasted past us at the start of the final straight, going on for his third win of the meet. Hawkard was by then nearly forty meters behind him, his stride short and choppy, his shoulders tight. He looked pathetic.

"Go Wally!" I yelled as he struggled towards us.

I was trying to be nice, but he didn't even glance up, and I felt a little bad for him. For a few seconds.

But then, as he made his way past us, his face red and angry, his intense blue eyes full of hate, that crease between his eyes looking like a headache made visible, I remembered that night three years before when he'd wished I was more of a dick. *Be careful what you wish for*, I'd told him.

I suddenly realized something. "So, what's the punchline?" I asked.

The kid looked confused. "It's that he kicks Hawkard's ass every race after the joke. That's the punchline. When he leaves him in the dust."

"No, I mean the punchline for the joke he just told him. The one about the guy trying to pee in the shot glass and instead peeing all over the bartender."

"Oh!" He grinned. "Oh yeah! Okay… So the bartender says, 'Why are you so happy? You just lost $1000!' and the guy says, 'Yeah, I just paid you $1000, but before I made that bet with you I bet that guy in the corner $10,000 I could piss all over you and you'd be happy about it!'"

I laughed out loud.

It was the best joke I'd heard in a long time.

Miss Mamie by Maik Strosahl

She was always a big boned gal,
Raised on the river
To Jazz and gumbo,
Crawdads and
Gambling men with big cigars
Who came with their taste for tobacco
Only bested by liquor and
Women willing to take them in
For silver.

Oh, but Miss Mamie,
She don't play that way,
She just float across the waters,
She just paddle across the Mississip,
Waving to the children along the shore.

She was always a proud woman
Dressed for visitors,
Dinner dances where
The sun would fade
And the waters grow black,
But she wore lights like diamonds
That sparkled through the night
And she could be seen
Whistling around the bend,
Singing the blues to a crowd
Too drunk to appreciate her,
Too involved in pairs and straights
And a good smoke.

But these are only memories –
The men went chasing for gold,
Women went chasing for their crumbs,
The river flooded
And when it returned to its place
She was left alone ashore,
A shell of her former self.

She has always been big boned,
But those bones
Were born to float,
Not to dry and rot into the soil.

We found her bones,
Imagined them
Lit up again with diamonds,
Jazz band still playing,
Poker still being dealt,
Men still filled with smoke and drink,
Women still laughing for tips
As her paddle pushes black waters,
Steam still whistling around the bend.

One day,
By the light of the morning sun,
She blazed away in a thick smoke
That carried Miss Mamie
Away to the clouds,
Big bones still floating
Upon the blue of an open sky.

Along The White River by Alys Caviness-Gober

I Just Wanted a Beer by Steve VandeWater

My coworkers and I, one night we went out for a drink
After work and I'm the oldest in the group.
Those kids are all Gen Xers and Millennials I think.
I'm old and not considered "in the loop."

So anyway we went out to some place they all knew well
That brews its own concoctions on the spot.
I seldom go out drinkin' but I figured "what the Hell
I'll just get a Miller Lite and then a shot."

When the waiter dude came askin' what we all would like to drink
And I told him what I wanted, he just stared.
"We don't serve that here," he snorted as the kids all shook their
heads
"Our beer list's on those chalkboards over there."
By the time I got done lookin' at the beers there on that list
My vision it was blurred, my mind confused.
Not one of them I recognized, it really made me pissed
I was feelin' like my brain had been abused.

There was Dortmunder, Vienna Lager, Weizenbier & Gose
And somethin' called a Tripel Belgian Ale.
There was Porter, Kolsch, and Dunkel, Helles, Rauchenbier, all those
And everything from Bitter Dark to Pale.

I finally saw a Pils, which I figured was the same
As the Pilsner Miller Lite has claimed to be.
So I ordered that one from the guy who put me to such shame
But it tasted like a glass of cloudy pee.

Now I do not know a Saison from a Chocolate Oatmeal Stout
Or a Barley Wine from Marzen, Bock, or Wit.
And I don't know what a Scotch Ale or a Lambic's all about
But I do believe it's all a crock o' shit.

I'll keep passing by those brewpubs all along my daily drive
Let the skinny, bearded, Hipsters act like boors.

I'll just confine my drinkin' to my fav'rite local dive
Where I get the normal stuff like Bud and Coors.

But everything comes back again after it's out of style
And my fav'rites will again take center stage.
I'll be lookin' really cool then, 'cause I drank it all the while
These young turds and microbrews were all the rage.

The Good, The Bad, and The But I Don't Wanna by Alys Caviness-Gober

The Good ~

Blooming roses in the Spring
and a yellow butterfly dancing
to the tune of bird songs
all summer long
leaves whispering in the trees
then falling gently in the Fall
amidst the still-soft kisses of the wind

poems that come complete
composed in Latin in my mind
as I sleep and when awake
once translated still works
paintings that appear on canvas
as if by magic the layers of my visions
recognizable

Books that read me to sleep
and stay forever in my dreams
movies that pierce my heart
with joy or aching everlasting
beloved faces smiling talking
or just sitting silently here
at our table and in my memories

The Bad ~

Numbed moments and lost days
without ease or kindness
feverish ruminations running
within fevers that run too often too high
Pain thundering on in
oppressive iron weights
upon my chest

Forgotten words and names
elusively flit at the edges
of this leaky sieve of a brain
take a breath (will the word come through this time?)
When "the first one" means
there's more and
despairing after each

Off balance
knocking over and into
everything peripheral
coffee spills regularly
as my hand hits my cup
I really do walk into doors
and cupboards and even walls

The But I Don't Wanna ~

get up
pay attention
do laundry
clean (anything)
cook (anything)
see (anyone)
go (anywhere)

think
speak
move

or wear real clothes
cuz my *'merz*
(flannel shirts & pajama pants)
are so damn comfy

The *but I don't wanna* days
slip in
quietly like a cat burglar
but the aftermath is
total devastation

irreplaceable items
(my precious days)
stolen
a hurricane's destruction

I live in the Eye of the Storm

I Should've by Vivian Belle

I should've killed him straightaway. Well, by straightaway I mean as soon as he showed his true colors. I mean, you don't always see true colors right away, you know? Sure as Hell they don't warn you of the true colors downside, do they? Rat bastards. It's all light and love and rainbows and slobbery kisses, to hear them tell you what it'll be like. Gosh-durned liars! I mean, if I'd've known then what the next 15 years of Hell and hardship and mess and worry and wreckage and expense would be like, yes, I'd've opted for murder straight-damn-away. Murder in the first degree with malice aforethought or whatever. Some might've called it self-defense, which is kinda a constitutional right, but I won't quibble. Murder'll do. I mean, I've seen all the seasons of *Wentworth* and *Orange Is The New Black* and I think I'd've been okay if I'd've got caught.

Which begs the question, would I have got caught?? Let's go with *NO*. I mean, sure, it's possible I'd've got caught, but honestly ~ and I'm admitting to nothing here ~ honestly, having gone over a thousand and one scenarios in my mind over these 30-odd years since then, I'm pretty sure I wouldn't've got caught. I mean, I've thought out an awful lot of murderous detail in the past 30-odd years, okay? Like, forensically, okay? At least 984 of my thousand and one scenarios left no evidence whatsoever, so I honestly believe there's no way I'd've got caught.

Still, if I ever get caught – I mean, if I ever would've got caught – and I'm not really admitting that possibility ~ but if I ever would've got caught, I'd've been okay with that. It'd be totally worth it. Seriously, I mean, even if I'd've got caught, been charged, been found guilty, and been transported off to whatever Hell-hole they wanted to stick me in "after committing my special crime," as Arlo would say, I wouldn't mind. Besides, I look *GREAT* in orange.

Scenes from Nowhere Town by Jenny Kalahar

As he spoons oatmeal into his mouth with a shaking hand,
I comb his hair, detangling it from yellowish clumps of memories
that have seeped from his pores overnight
until his hair lies smooth again,
gray with a sheen and shine
that comes from conditioning it with dreams

Before afternoon tea, I wipe his brow and temples
dry his cheeks where lost thoughts have dribbled
have settled into wrinkles at his forehead.
And we talk as best we can, keeping conversation
to the long ago
far away
to the dead who seem to be still alive to my father
childhood friends I never knew
his wife I called my mother
who lost him in her own mind
before she left us in body

Having no children, I fear the years to come
knowing this family affliction may also claim me.
Who will be my compassionate companion?
Who will comb out my tangles as I spoon up oatmeal,
wipe my cheeks dry of the things I will lose

drop by drop?
I will be alone in a way no one should be alone
when even their fondest memories

and their hopes
have been left behind on a yellowing pillowcase
in a too-quiet bedroom
at the edge of Nowhere Town

Assassin Lvl 17 by Bryony Stanger

Calling Out To Me by Michael Stewart
(*song lyric*)

My guitar has always been by my side through thick and thin
And when I need to find a friend it's always – Calling out to me
But I haven't played in many years in a place where everybody hears
Your mistakes and sees your fears stage fright – Calling out to me
But could I ever find the nerve to dig down deep in my reserve
And find out what I have preserved it's faintly – Calling out to me

Now when I hear these callings don't know how long they will last
But I'm paying more attention with less future than past
They're sometimes hard to understand they come and go so fast
But calling – Calling out to me

My darling wife is just the best brings me joy and happiness
And in a voice I like more than the rest softly – Calling out to me
I really miss my family spread out way too far to see too
Often I wish they could be closer and – Calling out to me
But when I get to see my friends hang out where no one pretends
To up the score or further ends harmony – Calling out to me

Now when I hear these callings don't know how long they will last
But I'm paying more attention with less future than past
They're sometimes hard to understand they come and go so fast
But calling – Calling out to me

Calling out to me calling out to me calling out to me calling out to me

I did some things back in my youth rude crude unfair uncouth
But I've learned to accept the truth penitence – Calling out to me
I'm trying to be an upright man 'tis of thee for which I stand
Counted as a helping hand hometown – Calling out to me
But every time I go to town let all my defenses down
Play the fool and act the clown my vices – Calling out to me

Calling out to me calling out to me calling out to me calling out to me

The Grass Is Aways Greener by Leslie Ober

A Sojourner's Truths *by Deborah Petersen*
(a 2018 *NICE* entry, inspired by *Follow the River*)

I. A Journey from Here to There

Planned and packed, focused and moving
Straight or circuitous path
Easy, carefree or bruising and blisters
What makes it a sojourn and not just motion
Is the appreciation
The awareness
The gratitude
The thankfulness
The sharpened senses at the ready, the ready to experience it all – to
be molded.

II. A Journey of Becoming

Diving in, deep
Vision past forgiveness
Light beacons only when you are able to withstand the brilliance
A language without words
Epiphany of understanding
These, and a wisdom of the ages pave this path of self-realization.

Physical, spiritual-
After all
is defined by ultimate path
Each by the grace and blessing
To the **Coming Home** – the Truth and Destination of Each Sojourn.

What You Don't Know by John Gilmore
(*song lyric*)

They say what you don't know can't hurt you
And I guess that that might be true
But there's things that you don't know
that damned sure hurt me
and there's nothing that I can do
Nothing that I can do now
but stand here and just watch you go
there's so much I wish I could tell you
but I don't think that you'd want to know

Like what all I'd do to make you love me
or where in my daydreams we go
or how much I think about you dear
I don't think that you'd want to know

They say what you don't know can't hurt you
and I guess that that might be right
so you just go on not knowing
while I sing my sad songs tonight
Sittin' alone with my thoughts now
and a heartache that I can't let show
oh, there's so much I wish I could tell
but I know that you don't want to know

Like how it hurts to want someone
you know can never be yours
or what causes such pain as love in vain
I know that you don't want to know
and I hope that you don't ever know

Like how it hurts to want someone
you know can never be yours
or what causes such pain as love in vain
I know that you don't want to know
and I hope that you don't ever know

Tomato Aspic by Sarah E. Morin

First off, it was the name.
As-pic.
"Carolyn, love of my life,
I'm not going to eat something that sounds like I'm picking a
wedgie."

She kissed the S-shaped crease between my eyebrows.
"Good, you shouldn't pick wedgies in public."
Which had nothing to do with anything
and I still had to eat the aspic.

Fruit-flavored Jell-o
wobbling
down
your
throat
like a live lime-flavored fish,
bad enough.
But cold tomato Jell-o?
Acid-sweet, with things that didn't belong in self-respecting tomato
dishes,
cloves and lemon juice.
My wife smuggled them in with the glee of a 1st grader let loose to
make her own PBJ,
only it became PB and gummy worm and crushed potato chip while
Mom's back was turned.

But the worst part was the ring mold Carolyn poured it in.
She'd set it out on the counter.
It excited me.
I earned a Bundt cake for unjamming the paper shredder.
I always served myself 2 slices of her Bundt cake because hey,
a cake with a hole in it is only half the calories.
But no, the kitchen filled with the incongruous smell of vegetable
soup.
It was unfair, got your hopes up.
Like how Garfield the Cat hates oatmeal raisin cookies

'cause they look like chocolate chip cookies
from a distance.

"My flower, do you have to use the Bundt pan?
It's false advertising."

"Yes, dear, that's where the shrimp goes."

Yeah, in the hole.
She poured chilled shrimp in the hole of the tomato aspic Bundt,
which only increased the sensation of live fish
wriggling
down
your
throat.
They were the kind of shrimp with no shell but the tails still on,
which made them look half-dressed:
a school of semi-nude crustaceans swarming from a wobbling blood-
colored mound.
I hated tomato aspic in more ways than I could describe.

But Carolyn loved it.
She made it every time company came over,
set it in the middle of the table like a centerpiece of potted flowers.
It traumatized the children.
No one ate much of it,
except Carolyn
and me
because she made us eat the leftovers for a week.

With husbandly tact and whining I persuaded her.
Eventually, she tomato aspicked only once a year.
The family potluck.
I think they tipped it into the cow field when we'd gone.
I watched the kitchen counter a full week before the annual potluck
so the moment the Bundt pan appeared I could disappear
chased out of the house by deceptive, steamy vegetable soup wraiths.

Carolyn made tomato aspic every year of our wedded life
until last year

when she was in the hospital
eating other forms of Jell-o.
She died of breast cancer in January
shaky as gelatin.

Two days before the potluck
I sniffed the vacant kitchen,
as though haunting was a thing to be inhaled, detected through the
lungs.
I missed the tortured tomato ghosts.
Too late.
I had exorcised the aspic.

Her 1969 *Better Homes and Gardens* cookbook
smelled like apron and activism.
Her Post-it note, like a flag,
marked her presence in the pages.

2 envelopes unflavored gelatin.
Lemon juice.
2 bay leaves.
Carolyn bought a jar of bay leaves once a decade.
She never remembered to add them to her soup stock until too late
and when she did, never remembered to take them out.
If you found one in the bottom of your soup bowl, she cheered
like she'd arranged for you,
specifically you,
to receive the prize inside the cereal box.

Last,
the damn,
half-thawed,
shell-less,
shirtless,
semi-exposed shrimp.

I took it to the family potluck.
It was the first time we finished all the tomato aspic.
The last bite jiggled and giggled on my fork.
I heard the ghost of Carolyn snicker.

Lost Poems by W.B. Cornwell

She told me to take the poetry
Her mind was starting to fade
"Others would want it, it wasn't my place"
Is what I told myself, so I didn't . . .

I should have taken them
Had I known her children didn't really care
Had I known it would end up at a landfill
Had I known it would be lost forever
I would have taken them home . . .

Her words, her thoughts a part of her soul
Gone! It is all gone!
I am thankful for what I had copied
I am thankful for the published ones I've found
Still, the lost poems haunt me . . .

On paper written by hand
Others typed on a typewriter, long since forgotten
Paper stained with drops of coffee
Stained with menthol cigarette smoke, having yellow hues
Papers bent and folded, stapled and hole punched

Unfinished works, first drafts of pieces that were published
Her words, her thoughts, a part of her soul
Gone! It is all gone!
And always the lost poems will haunt me . . .

Two Little Owls by Patty Hunter
(a 2018 *NICE* entry, inspired by *Follow the River*)

Two little owls
sitting in the woods,
Sleeping and eating
As little owls should

Cute as a button
both of them are,
sweet, yet strong
when seen from afar

Oh, the two little owls
Are just babies, you see
Just like two little fluffed balls,
if you please.

Two little owls
Learning to fly
with their mother
From way up high

Oh, the two little owls
Are just babies, you see
Just like two little fluffed balls,
if you please.

But, soon they'll grow
To be big and strong
To be the kings of the woods
To hunt all year round.

Oh, the two little owls
Are just babies, you see
Just like two little fluffed balls,
if you please.

Labyrinth Slot Canyon by Danika Geisler
(Lake Powell, Utah)

Columbus Georgia 1971 by Alys Caviness-Gober

In spite of my braided pigtails corralling my thick long blonde hair,
sweat drips from my hairline down into my eyes. I feel the sweat
trickle down my back, the scratchy fabric of my blue and white
checkered dress sticking uncomfortably to my back; the backs of my
knees are wet with sweat.

I'm standing on the sidewalk outside the front doors of my Columbus,
Georgia elementary school, in my usual spot where I say bye to my
friends before I walk home. Today's not usual, though.

The midday sun burns white and I squint; this isn't the usual time of
day to leave school. My always-oh-so-confusing 3rd grade math class
ended abruptly about 30 minutes ago when the school-bell clanged
unexpectedly ~ we all jumped out of our skins ~ and our new teacher
announced that the entire school is dismissed. I like our new teacher;
she smells like the roses in our backyard rose garden.

Now, I stand bewildered and embarrassed on the scorching white
concrete. I'm transfixed with something that feels very much like
fear. I watch as my classmates are pulled by their arms by their angry
parents, their parents walk fast and pull my friends behind them. My
friends stumble awkwardly to keep up. Their parents are scowling,
some are stomping silent, some are shouting. Tommy, a friend of
mine, he's in my math class, gets dragged past me by his mother; her
pale white face contorts like a movie-monster's face ~ red, sweaty,
twisted, eyes flaring wildly.

She shouts, *"Ain't no son of mine gonna be taught by no NIGGER!"*

My friend Tommy is crying. I feel sick to my stomach.

I continue to feel sick to my stomach as I walk home; instead of the
sidewalks that go around several streets ~ blocks of large-lot (ie, large
front and back yards) single-family residential properties ~ I take the
fastest route home, across the football field of the Junior High. The
field separates my school from the Junior High, where I know I'll go
in a few short years. There's a narrow band of forest ~ tall Georgia
pines ~ that runs the length of the football field and school property.

On the other side of the forest are several blocks of our residential area. At one corner of the football field there's the top of a long concrete path, bordered on each side by a house with large front and back yards. The concrete path runs downhill between the houses to my street; our house is directly across the street from the bottom of the concrete path. I'm walking fast, faster than normal. I want to get home. I'm practically running, I'm walking so fast, determined to get to that concrete path that leads to our house.

I walk to school going up the concrete path each morning, and I always stop at the top and turn to wave to my mom, who watches me make it safely to school property. Even back then, the world was a scary place, I guess. Home feels safe, though. Home for me back then was lots of trips to doctors (I have a rare lung disease), and books and old movies. Life was in my head, mostly ~ the real world was "out there" somewhere far away and sometimes I didn't quite understand it. Walking home this day, I feel confused and sick and scared. I think about before we moved to Georgia, when lived in San Diego. I liked our apartment life, there were lots of kids living in the apartments. I remember playing with all the kids ~ I don't notice or care that some of them have different colored skin thank I do. I don't yet know labels like blacks, Mexicans, etc. This day, I think about all those kids. I think about Tommy and Tommy's mother. I think: keep your head down, get home, feel safe. The Georgia heat and humidity aren't helping my sick feeling.

The Deep South in late May and early June is unbearably hot, with a thickness that seems more like floating liquid rather than air. From May to July in 1971, the heat and humidity seemed to be a choking metaphor for my city's mood. During those months, Georgia erupted with Civil Rights protests, protests by blacks against discrimination, especially by the police, and protests by whites against integration, especially school integration. A State of Emergency was declared by peanut-farmer-turned-Governor Jimmy Carter. The first Supreme Court decision in the *Brown v. Board of Education* case had happened in 1954, and the second Supreme Court decision in *Brown*, the one that said integration must occur "with all deliberate speed" was handed down by the Court in 1955, but most of the Deep South didn't recognize either rule of law for years. Columbus was no exception. By the time Jimmy Carter was elected Governor of Georgia in 1970, blacks and whites were still segregated ~ by neighborhoods, by businesses, by churches, and of course by schools.

The morning that the first African-American teacher sat behind a desk at my grade school, the day Tommy's mother dragged him past me, was in 1971. Little did I know that in the months and years to come, that experience would be repeated as buses from black neighborhoods, buses filled with black kids, rolled up to my elementary school and Junior High schools for the first times. The day Tommy's mother screamed the n-word so publicly was just the first of my memories of some racially-charged ugly days, but, on that one day when I was almost eight-years-old, I'd never experienced anything quite like what I saw, felt, and heard that day.

My family wasn't from the Deep South. My dad was born and raised in Oregon. He joined the US Navy right out of High School and traveled the world in uniform during the Korean War. After he got out, he attended Portland State University on the GI Bill. My dad was the first person in his family to attend college. While he was at Portland State he met and married my mom. My mom was an immigrant. She born in Macedonia in 1939 (I don't think anyone in Georgia had ever heard of Macedonia). Mom came to America in 1940 with her older sister and their mother on the last passenger ship out of Europe for the duration of WWII. My mom was the first person in her family to attend college; she officially studied art, but she always made it clear that she, like many women of her generation, was there to earn her M-R-S degree. My folks were married in the Greek Orthodox church that my mom's family attended; that was the last church my parents ever set foot in.

Upon graduation from Portland State University, Dad was accepted into Cornell University's Grad School for psychology, and my folks moved to Ithaca, New York, where I was born. My dad earned his Master's and PhD in Psychology from Cornell University. He taught there, too. Cornell was the first university I attended; I remember as a toddler, perching upon a tall stool sitting at a table in front of the class near Dad's lectern. I sat quietly, a well-behaved child, coloring in my coloring books, while he taught the ins and outs of psychology to his students. Dad taught in universities as we lived, consecutively, in New York, Washington State, Oregon, and California. Education makes a difference in how you see the world and the people in it; higher education makes a huge difference.

By the time we lived in Georgia, Dad had changed careers and was a research psychologist for the Department of the Army. He did things like design psychological tests for incoming soldiers (you know, the kind of tests that let the Army know if you should be a sniper or a potato peeler). Dad used to have me take his tests, like some guinea pig. I didn't understand them (remember, I was just a kid!) and I have no idea what my "results" were (potato peeler? sniper?), but I didn't mind tests. I mean, tests were par for the course because I was born into an academically-minded family. I read anything I could get my hands on, going book by book through shelves at school and public libraries everywhere we lived. My parents used to tell me that they never knew anyone who had read as many books as I had, at any point in my life. Everything I knew about the world came from books. Reading was an easy escape for a sickly kid; books were more real to me than real life.

My family and my life with them made a difference in how I saw the world. When we moved to Georgia from southern California, it was crystal clear to me I didn't fit in (there weren't a lot of kids you'd call "readers"). It was equally clear my family didn't fit in. Religiosity is supreme in the South. People in Georgia are the *we're-all-God's-children Bible-thumping Christians* type and they go to church on Wednesday nights and twice on Sunday and we didn't go to church. At all. In fact, my folks happily explained to our well-meaning church-going Bible-thumping neighbors, who invited us to church services, that they didn't believe in organized religion. I think my folks expected people to be . . . tolerant. People weren't; they believed my parents worshipped the devil. It was embarrassing, to say the least.

Now, I had friends at school whose church-going Bible-thumping parents would offer to take me to church so that my immortal soul would be saved and I would not end up in Hell when I died (they were dead serious). Remember, I was between the ages of five and ten when we lived in Georgia, my death was imminent according to my doctors (my incurable rare lung disease prognosis was grim), and the thought of my immortal soul burning in Hell for all eternity scared the

Hell out of me. I *wanted* to go to church, I *wanted* my immortal soul to be saved. I thought it was really sweet of those good Christian *we're-all-God's-children Bible-thumping* folks to care so much about my immortal soul. They were clearly nice people who cared about every single person in the world. My parents graciously allowed me to go to various churches with my friends. Their churches didn't speak to my spiritual soul at all, but I was baptized several times over, every which way from river-dunkings to splashes of Holy Water. For my spiritual soul, I turned to my world mythology books, of which the Holy Bible was one ~ I don't mean that with any blasphemy or insult intended. To me, the Bible was just another book of religious stories, the mythology of a culture. Believe me, none of my Columbus Georgia friends wanted to hear that the Holy Bible was just a collection of mythological stories. Not attending church was Strike One against us; to the good Christian *we're-all-God's-children Bible-thumping* folks of Columbus Georgia attending church and "being" Christianity were not optional.

Strike Two was that we were vegetarian health food nuts who didn't eat out, even for fast food, let alone a real restaurant. A lot of Southern women took pride in their meat-centered home cooking, and they also enjoyed the occasional restaurant or fast food meal. To them, my mom's homemade granola and homemade yogurt (made from a from-scratch homemade-starter) was hippy-dippy devil food.

Strike Three was: we ran. On foot. For those of you who are confused, I mean we literally ran for miles and miles. Us kids (my two brothers were born in Georgia) ran at least 6.7 miles per day, either before or after school. Mom ran about 8 miles a day; Dad ran 15-20 miles *on his lunch hour* at Fort Benning. Every evening at 5:15pm sharp, he walked into our house expecting dinner to be on the table ~ because of his running at lunch time, he hadn't eaten since his hippy-dippy devil food granola and yogurt for breakfast. We all wore Frank Shorter running gear as regular clothes. This was before wearing celebrity-endorsed clothing was a thing and before wearing yoga pants or any kind of athletic wear as regular clothes was a thing. (In fact, I don't think yoga pants had been invented yet.) As kids, we had the newest designs of Puma, Nike, Adidas, New Balance, and Reebok running shoes practically right as they came off the manufacturing lines. Our family was weird because running was all we did. We didn't have other hobbies or family activities. We just ran. We ran our training runs every day, and we ran road races on weekends. My dad was fast and my little brothers both ended up pretty good runners; I was abysmal, but that was understandable. Remember, I did (and still do) have a rare incurable lung disease; running *sucked* for me. Anyway, running was everything in our family. No one we knew understood why we ran; they just thought it was weird. Back then, folks in Georgia, and almost everywhere else, didn't run for fun or even for fitness. Some High School and College kids ran track, but that's it.

So, to everyone else, I was part of a strange hippy-dippy devil-worshipping-vegetarian-health-nut-food-eating-running-for-no-good-reason family. They knew I didn't have fried chicken for Sunday supper after church, they knew I didn't go to church at all, and they knew I did other stuff that was odd: my nose was always stuck in a book, I called the last meal of the day dinner, and I liked to talk about far-off places and peoples and world religions that I'd read about in my books.

And then there was Strike Four ~ worst of all ~ which was that in the schoolyard at recess and in the city library and in the city parks, I'd wander over and talk to and sit with nigger kids just as much as I'd sit with and talk to white kids. Parks, by the way, like almost everything else, were still formally segregated in Georgia back then. I think I was the only kid, of either color, to cross sides. I crossed from our part (the white part) to the nigger side. Now, let me say right here that I did not ever use the n-word: nigger kids is what every Christian *we're-all-God's-children church-going Bible-thumping* white adult and white kid I knew in Columbus Georgia called the African-American kids in town, and nigger side is what Christian *we're-all-God's-children church-going Bible-thumping* white adults and white kids in Columbus, Georgia called anywhere the African-Americans lived, worked, played, worshipped ~ anywhere not our part, "not white." I didn't like hearing those *n*-words then and I don't like using them now, but this is a true story, so I'm keeping it real, as they say.

Keeping it real, keeping it real. Well, okay. I didn't go to any African-American churches with any of my African-American school friends. Those kids were just as worried about my immortal soul as my white friends were, but our friendships were limited to school. My African-American school friends didn't invite me to go to church, because no matter how much I talked with them or sat with them or played with them at recess, I wasn't one of them, and they all knew they couldn't invite me to their homes or churches. I mean, sure, they "could have," like if we were living in some modern-day movie with a mythological (rewritten history) storyline about a seminal friendship between a white kid and an African-American kid in the Deep South in the late 1960s/early 1970s or something, but in the real world? No, they couldn't have. They knew better. Segregation causes barriers that are invisible and unconquerable for most adults, let alone children.

I didn't really understand the near-100% segregation of Columbus back then, because even as young as I was, I knew that there were neighborhoods in other states where whites/blacks were integrated; I knew there were integrated parks and schools all over the country. I remembered San Diego apartment life. I didn't know the words back then, but I knew my family was not a family of racist intolerant bigots, like our white Christian *we're-all-God's-children church-going Bible-thumping* neighbors in Georgia. I didn't know the words back then, but I knew we were what I now know is called liberal, progressive, tolerant, and educated.

I get home from school that hot hopeless helpless day in 1971, and my dad is *home* and *the TV is on in the dining room*. I think, what is going on today?? because: 1) our little black and white portable TV is kept in the linen closet and only brought out for special annual things like the Academy Awards and *Gone With The Wind*, and 2) my dad gets home from work every day exactly at 5:15pm. Mom always has dinner on the table by 5:30pm. Why is Dad home at midday?? Why is the TV on??

I ask my dad what is going on; I expect him to say something to make me feel better. My dad tells me about all the bad race-related things happening in the news. I tell him about my 3rd grade math class ending abruptly and the school-bell clanging unexpectedly and how we all jumped out of our skins and I tell him about the entire school being dismissed and me standing bewildered on the scorching white concrete and I tell him about Tommy and Tommy's mother.

My father then tells me:

White people here don't think like we do about black people, but you have to act like the white people here. Don't say anything about what you really think or how you really feel. You have to act like they do. I mean it, Alys.

My whole childhood, whenever my dad said *I mean it*, that was rule of law. So, at almost eight years old, I had my marching orders. They turned my world upside down.

That day in 1971 when I was almost eight years old and sick of 3rd grade, I was ready for the slow days of summer to start, and all I really cared about was that my birthday was in June, the next month. That whole day, that whole experience, changed me from the self-oriented birthday-anticipating child to something quite different. Although I had no words at the time for how I felt, it was the first time I felt, for lack of a better phrase, race shame ~ in today's vernacular, white privilege. I stood on that scorching concrete, dripping in the sweat of not just the weather but also my emotions, and I was embarrassed to be white. Because even at age not-quite eight years old, I knew I didn't want to be equated with white people like Tommy's mother.

As the months and years passed, integration happened slowly and with great ugliness. My grade school and Junior High years in Columbus (we moved to Noblesville when I was in 7th grade), were marred and scarred by days where school was dismissed abruptly and early because of racial tensions. In the mornings, when the buses pulled up filled with African-American kids, who, by the way, were forced to come to "white" schools by "forced integration" policies, there were always school officials (and sometimes police) escorting the Africa-American kids into the building. And there was always a line of cars driven by irate white parents, pulling their kids out of school. I guess those parents thought the schools would buckle and stop letting in the African-America kids. But even in Georgia, the law was the law, and it didn't matter how many white kids got taken home by their racist parents: integration was the law. Our schools eventually stopped having abrupt early dismissals. Slowly but surely, things settled down, and at least on the surface, schools were integrated.

I often wonder what that day did to Tommy ~ did he grow up to be a David Duke? Did he have kids that he raised to be racist? I hope not; I hope he broke the cycle, but the odds were never in his favor. In the years that followed, Tommy and I stayed friends as classmates, but we never talked about that day. Looking back, I try to imagine how he felt that day. Back then, boys weren't supposed to cry or show much emotion, but I saw his face as his mother dragged him past me.

I wonder about our 3rd grade math teacher, the one who smelled of roses. My mother smelled of *Shalimar*, my grandmother's scent was *Emeraude*; to this day, I wish I had asked my teacher the name of her perfume. But I never did. I don't remember her much more than as she was that scorching hot day in 1971. I remember her face. At the time, as an almost-eight-year-old, I thought she looked really serious. Now I realize that she was a little bit scared and that she was fighting back tears. I wonder whatever happened to her.

And what about my dad? My marching orders that day were *to follow the herd, don't speak up, don't make waves*, especially not on behalf of others. It was the day my dad fell off a particular pedestal in my mind ~ one that represented honor and courage and doing what's right even when you know it's going to cause problems for yourself. Until that day, I thought my dad was like all the heroes and heroines in my books. I learned that day that love doesn't mean perfection. Pedestal or no pedestal, love is love. Perfection has nothing to do with it. At the time, as an almost-eight-year-old kid trying to grasp that conflicted concept, and realizing my dad wasn't the kind of man I thought he was, well, those were perhaps the worst things that happened to me that day. Of course, much later, after I had my own kids, I understood what my dad was really saying to me: *the world is dangerous, protect yourself, stay safe*. A parent's love and fear can outweigh honor and courage and doing the right thing because real parents aren't storybook characters.

Then there was my reaction to the white Christian *we're-all-God's-children church-going Bible-thumping* folks, the types who wanted to take me to their churches to save my (white) immortal soul whilst they called other human beings *niggers*. It was the day I understood the word hypocrisy in real terms. I'd read the Bible, I knew what Jesus allegedly said. Above all these is Love, right? But for white

Christian *we're-all-God's-children church-going Bible-thumping* folks, for them, Jesus did not mean, "love *niggers*."

That day, I realized that all those myths and stories from world cultures that I'd been reading, including those in the Holy Bible, were a huge part of what ruled human behaviors. They get used; the admonitions and lessons and preachings that came out of churches make people intolerant and racist and hate-filled. The clash between purported white Christian loving kindness and Tommy's mother's hate-twisted face screaming ugly words scarred me for life, and definitively ended any desire I had to go to any church. It was clear to me that day that if I had to go a church to make sure my (white) immortal soul was saved before I died, well, then I'd just as soon head on off to Hell when my time came.

Everything that happened at school and at home that day caused the end of certain innocences for me: it shook my white-skinned comfort zone, it shook my perception of my father, and it shook my faith and trust in other people, particularly many who claim to be Christian. It was the beginning of other things, too, things I couldn't verbalize at the time or understand for many years. Reading everything I could get my hands on became not just the easy escape of a sickly kid; reading became educationally important, world-view important. That day eventually led me to study world cultures in college, and to teach at the University level. Later, still rejecting the hypocrisies of organized religions, I formed a non-denominational spiritual ministry that celebrates a little bit from a lot of world religions (without holding formal church services). It was the beginning of me trying to stand up, to advocate for and understand anyone labeled as "other" than me; I haven't always been as courageous in that area as I wish, but I try. That day also caused me to develop a character trait that doesn't serve very well in the real world: an overly-honed sense of injustice. (Man, that can really bite you in the ass in the real world! But, those are stories for another day.). Like most memories, that one day in Columbus, Georgia in 1971 was then and remains for me now layered, nuanced, and complicated. To borrow from Charles Dickens, looking back on it now, it was one of both the best of times and the worst of times in my childhood.

Schism II by Alys Caviness-Gober

The Storm Demands by Nancy Simmonds
(a 2018 *NICE* entry, inspired by *The Three Musketeers*)

It is not possible to sip of a storm

while poised, buttoned, and reserved
every hair in place
modulated tones in calm conversation
little finger raised just so
in a clean and well-darned glove

the chance remark a whisper,
acknowledged only by the trembling
of the ostrich plume on her hat.

No.

A storm demands

a pounding heart
a bodice button slipping free of its tightly stretched hold
half-moons of fingernail marks fading in the sweat of her palms

a tendril of hair
tumbling free
sticking to a neck slick with perspiration
cording in the tight reins of restraint

a jagged crack of lightning in the sky
mirroring the break in her heart.

Despair

tightly corseted by the good manners of polite society
howls and growls

burns in silence
until the blackbird guests have flown
the servants clear away
the door is gently closed

and she is left alone.

Feeling Trapped by Leslie Ober

A Difficult Life by Vivian Belle

One

Most of the other kids at school are mean. There are a few quiet ones who are nice. I think they just hope the mean kids won't see them, though, so I guess maybe they are not really nice. They seem nice, because they're quiet and they don't even look at me. I don't care if they aren't really nice and I wouldn't care if they look at me; I mean, I get it – that'd just bring attention to them and to me and the mean kids would just start in on all of us. I sometimes hope the mean kids won't see me but they usually do, no matter how quiet I am and I don't like to be quiet. I like to sing and dance and recite movie scenes; Mother loves my singing and dancing and acting out movie scenes. She always asks me to perform when her friends come for lunch. I dress in fabulous bits of Mother's lovely clothes and my makeup is better than a movie star's and I sing and dance and act for Mother's friends. Most of them are nice and applaud and smile; some look confused and won't look Mother or me in the eye but their eyes are like stupid pig-slits. I don't care; the others love me, they love my performances. Mother loves my performances.

My favorite thing is to draw and paint, and at school I hate everything else especially the stupid sports games, so I guess I am not really surprised when some of the other kids are mean to me – that's just what happens when you don't like the same stuff they like. They push me around in the hallways and pull my curls and knock my books out of my arms. The nuns don't care. They just watch severely, their eyes always watching everything. The mean kids shout at me: *"Hey ooh-ooh-ooh girl!"* and laugh at me. I know they are really just kinda mad because they aren't as special as I am – I win all the Art awards, and they don't have my curly hair and flashing eyes. Their hair is weird and flat and their eyes are like stupid pig-slits – even when they laugh, their eyes don't laugh. I have a much prettier mouth than any of them. You've never seen such awful lips as theirs, too – like a rhinoceros' ankle. Oh sure, their clothes might be made out of all the right patterns and materials, but I have the nicest shoes. My shoes are perfect. They have white soles and lovely laces, and the tops are a fine deep blue, much darker than the cornflowers growing wild over by the railroad tracks. No matter what they do to me, I tell myself, *My shoes are perfect.* After that, it really doesn't matter what happens.

Two

I move out and away from Mother's house. I live in sophistication; I am sophistication, alive and pulsing in a metropolis, not stuck in the backwoods. Art school has me enthralled, for the teachers are awed by my talent. They all praise me, my new beautiful prestigiously titled artistic teachers – all the time they praise me, saying *"how lovely"* and *"oh! remarkable!"* Their eyes always watch me with delight. They pet me and give me tea and cookies and speak of nurturing me and my Art. They all want to nurture me. On clear bright days, they take me to all the right galleries, and they speak bright promises of nurturing my Art, so that someday my Art can hang in those very galleries. In the star-twinkled nights, they take me to the operas and the theaters and the cinemas and they compare my loveliness to that of the beautiful stars of stage and screen. Each day is sophistication itself, clear and bright, and after the red sinking sunsets, they nurture me through the star-twinkled nights. I am just about nurtured to death by them, as night after night ends in the wee small hours, in their cozy private rooms, and their eyes gleam like stupid pig-slits. They nurture me so much and so often and I neglect my Art because I have no time and they are all nurturing me.

Then, after I've had no time for my Art because of all their nurturing, their fawning words dry up and fizzle away. They tell me that my Art has left me. They say I have failed my Art, in spite of all their nurturing. They complain about all the time they wasted nurturing me and my Art. They say they don't want to nurture me anymore – no more tea and cookies, no more galleries, operas and theaters and cinemas, no more nurturing in their cozy private rooms, but I don't care. As if their fawning words have anything to do with my Artistic reality! They won't know Art if it jumps in their lap and kisses them! They may have all the prestigious titles, and they may frequent all the right galleries and operas and theaters and cinemas, but I have the nicest shoes. My shoes are perfect. They have white soles and lovely laces, and the tops are a fine deep blue, much darker than the cornflowers growing wild down by the railroad tracks. No matter what they do to me, I tell myself, *My shoes are perfect.* After that, it really doesn't matter what happens.

Three

I live in paradise now, with my darling. He is perfectly wonderful – truly beautiful. He says I am the loveliest thing he has ever seen. I take that as quite a compliment because he is in the movie business! He's seen many a starlet come and go, and he's even met some of the most handsome and powerful men in Hollywood. He tells me all the time that I will be a great star. He's worked with quite a few big stars, too, so when he says he loves my curly hair and flashing eyes, well, I know he means it. He says, *"your mouth is – my god, your lips are so – they will make a fortune!"* Not since Dorothy Lamour, he says, has Hollywood seen lips like mine. He tells me how he will help me break into the movie business. He tells me many stories about how hard it is to find just the right project, just the right people to help you. He says so many beautiful lovelies like me make the mistake of trusting people who turn out to be the wrong people. He says trust should only be given to the one who truly loves you. He tells me how much he loves me.

One day, early, with the light still sleepy and gray, he wakes me and says, *"today, today is the day you become a star!"* We drive away, into the gray dawn for a long time we drive, and I fall back asleep. He wakes me again, *"we're here."* Here is where I will become a star. I am sleepy like the sky, but up the stairs we go. The room is dark and gray like the dawn when I awoke. He tells me that he is the only person I can trust. He tells me he loves me and that these men are his friends and that our project will be Number One around the world. He tells me that I will become a great star, and his friends will help me. It is nice of them to help me, he tells me, because they know I have no experience in the movie business – they are taking a big chance on me, he tells me. *Trust me*, he says, *because only I love you*. The men start to act with me, over and over, one and then another and then another and another and I see my darling's eyes always watch me. Light comes and goes, as the men act with me, over and over, one after another. Sometimes I feel like I am dying, but his eyes always watch me. I see his eyes watching me. The project takes many hours and the men do not speak to me. I never hear their names; they leave.

We drive away, into the gray twilight, a silent light, and the drive is long and I am dying a little and I fall asleep. He wakes me, and says, "*get out.*" I get out, thinking we are home, but the street is not familiar to me. I watch as his car drives away into the gray dusk. I think about his words of love and trust and his promises. I think about our project and his eyes like pig-slits always watching me and I think of his friends, doing me a favor with all their movie business experience, and I remember the light coming and going as they acted with me. I see the stars twinkle up in the sky and I know he's seen many a starlet and he's met some handsome and powerful men in Hollywood, and he's worked with quite a few big stars, but I have the nicest shoes. My shoes are perfect. They have white soles and lovely laces, and the tops are a fine deep blue, much darker than the cornflowers growing wild around the railroad tracks. No matter what they do to me, I tell myself, *My shoes are perfect*. After that, it really doesn't matter what happens.

Four
I did not want to come here and I do not belong here and they should just let me go. I think I am supposed to meet someone later – he could be "*the one,*" you know, the one who truly understands my Art. I don't want to be late. I have to do my hair. I don't like these people, so I will not talk to them. They keep saying a name at me, loudly, but it is not my name. They are loud, so loud, their voices pound into my ears like railroad spikes and they keep asking me questions: "*Do you know where you are? Do you know why you are here? Do you*

remember anything?" I don't like the way they look at me. I will not answer their questions. They destroyed my Art when they wrapped it like a mummy with their stupid white cloth strips – how could they do that?! I can barely see the red through the white strips of cloth, the red of my Masterpiece, the red like the deep-dawning sun after a gray twilight and a dark night, the red like the sinking sun after a clear bright day. They destroy my Art with their stupid white strips of cloth and their loud voices.

One of them wears a mask. Behind his mask, his mouth moves, but I don't really see his lips – he probably has lips like a rhinoceros' ankle. Above his mask, his eyes always watch me. His eyes are pig-slits pretending to be nice. All of these white-dressed people – I do not trust them, they do not love me, they are strangers. I know they must be crazy – nobody wears white this time of year. They think they are so smart in their white, but I have the nicest shoes. My shoes are perfect. They have white soles and lovely laces, and the tops are a fine deep blue, much darker than the cornflowers growing wild against the railroad tracks. No matter what they do to me, I tell myself, *My shoes are perfect.* After that, it really doesn't matter what happens.

Five

All the way across the country, a telephone rings in a kitchen. An older woman walks to the phone. She is tall, and grace fills her, moving like a softened day. She, too, has curly hair. It is gray and lovely and her eyes flash. She has a beautiful mouth. She answers, *"Hello?"* She listens. *"Yes, I am she."* She listens. *"Yes."* She listens. *"Is it bad?"* She listens. *"Yes, yes, twice before. Please, tell him I'm coming."* She listens. *"Has he asked for me? Has he said anything?"* She listens. *"Oh."* Tears fall down her beautifully pale cheeks. *"Please, won't you tell him that I said he does have the most perfect shoes?"*

Out of The Box I by Alys Caviness-Gober

Summer of '17 by Maren Thornbury

The Summer of '17 was hot but wet and fast but slow in its moments.

It was the Summer of new beginnings . . . failed beginnings, but still new.

Seventeen was lost, sad, lonely, and afraid; and as March turned to April, and April to May, I found myself alone in my head once again . . .

The end of Spring felt more like death than rebirth.
It was the end of an era, end of the cycle I seemed to always fall into, and there was always a grace period before I learned to restart.

So Summer was dreaded, a rush of black sky I could wait to walk into . . .

but then there was you.

It could have started in a hot car on dirt roads, avoiding the highways while making long conversation about saving the world and windmills; listening to strange music I'd never heard before and the sun rising as my smile settled and you let me talk and talk and talk endlessly – like I was taught not to.

It could have started at a slumber party with new friends, painting your face and dancing to silly songs, playing games and giggling. Staying up till 4am so we could sit in the dark corner with candles and necklaces, talking to ghosts.

(You would insist later that you had been blowing on the chain we held, on the flame, that there were no ghosts, just you.
You are wrong.)

It could have started on a golf course, the sun long set and no flashlights. But there on the green and behind the trees the ghost was me, and you, and we all screamed in delight and ran through wet dew and slipped and fell and laughed so bright.
I remember feeling that maybe it was different this time, because it always felt different this time . . .
Autumn started so strong, with early mornings and schedules and smiles all around,
but slowly dry hot days turned to chilly wind advisories,
and planned outfits turned to pajama pants on a Wednesday,
and sleep was for the weak or at least the strong enough to not think past midnight.

Winter of '17 was cold and dark.
A black hole I could not see the exit, a void I could not climb out of, oh was the future a mass of anxiety and dread?
A spiral I would collapse inside over and over and over again . . . ?
Winter was full of white stale offices and needles stealing blood, starchy cotton dresses missing backs, and frustrated screams at five pm on a Tuesday.
Full of in-completes, dreaming through lesson plans, and sleeping through dinner.
Full of *I'm too sick to go*s and retching in bathroom mirrors,

of bringing a blanket to the toilet and making the cool tile my bed.
The teacher assigned us a paper and the question was happiness and I
did not have an answer.
Winter was a time of almost giving up, but I did not give up because .
. .

You taught me to think differently. Took my brain in your hands and
blew gently, changed the swing of things, kissed my head in just the
right spot . . .

this is what you want me to say, you want me to say that you saved
me, because that would mean you were special and that you meant
something.

You didn't save me though, he didn't save me! I saved me!

I took my melted head and stuck it in a freezer, I molded my face into
smiles and laughs, I took pen to paper and wrote my way out of the
darkness.
Turned that noose into a rope and hoisted the colors and sailed!
Sailed on thunderstorms into blue skies, bright lights at the end of
tunnels, and the future was no longer something to fear because
Fear is useless.
Him? He was on a raft back in space, lightning tracing the faces he
showed to anyone willing to look, all fake.

I saved myself.

The summer of '18 began slow and hazy and beautiful and happy, it
was the beginning of something extraordinary, something exciting.
It did not feel like false hope anymore, it felt real, it felt clear for the
first time.

Then the green skies turned brown and golden and red, the clouds
were on the ground and on fire and you,
oh you
ruined it.
Ha! You thought you ruined me?

I saved myself!

Maybe it started in the car, laughs and giggles and dirt roads, and idea forming, forming . . . brown hair bronze eyes crooked teeth; not girl, no, but tool, fool. Did you say, "I can fool her?"

I saved me

Maybe it started with ghosts, lies of lips and flickering flames . . . pretending to feel something, anything. Not spirits, just wind . . . but there was a ghost there, hiding in your smile and the *I love you*s you should have left at home.

Maybe it started on golf carts, bare feet, the darkness your favorite company, covers up deceit so you could so easily hide from me,

But I saved me

Maybe maybe
Screw maybe!
The truth will not set you free, for all we have is word of mouth and all you needed was belief.
Oh do I regret the memories of hazy smoky rooms we slept in? Of bottles shared and trips taken?
Regret the way I loved hard and strong and hopelessly?
My heart swollen, full, and my head smaller and pink and my arms open and my soft spoken words on foreign teeth?

Oh, no.
No I do not regret anything.

But God, do I wish I had known.

The First Time by Jo Mader

When someone says anything about "the first time," I don't think about my first day at school, or the first time I drove a car, or the first time I was kissed. I think of the opening line of this song:

> *"The first time ever I saw your face,*
> *I thought the sun rose in your eyes. . ."*

I spent the late 1960s and early 1970s on Army posts in Georgia. I sang with several different groups of women. At Fort Gordon, outside Augusta, our audiences were usually captive – young GIs in the orthopedic wards of the military hospital, which consisted of 144 interconnected Quonset huts built for the WWII generation. A Georgia summer in a tin-roofed hut is no one's idea of a good time.

So, we would go with our guitars and electric keyboards, amps and birthday cakes, cameras, pens and paper to write notes and take down the address of the Mom or the girlfriend that the picture of the birthday boy would go to after the film was developed. We provided a distraction to long, hot tedious days for young men wanting to be anywhere but where they were.

We sang rock classics, folk songs, the Birthday Song, Sinatra ballads, the Birthday Song, Scout camp sing-a-longs, *Amazing Grace* and a few other favorite hymns, the Birthday Song, most of the score from *My Fair Lady* and *Sound of Music*, and the Birthday Song.

On occasion, when requested, I would sing, *The First Time Ever I Saw Your Face*. It was popular that summer. We believed that if a soldier requested a love song, we should sing it.

We also believed he should have a hand to hold while he listened and thought about someone far away. That hand was mine. It was my "job" to sing it as a soloist, because I tipped the scales at 75 pounds and was the only one of us who could fit between two hospital beds less than a foot apart or manage to perch on a mattress next to wounded trooper with a casted leg in traction – without shaking the traction frame. We had performed it that way for over a year.

On a hot, sticky August afternoon, we arrived at the hospital and were told that this afternoon we wouldn't be singing on the wards. Because of the heat, the majority of orthopedic patients had been moved to a dining room that was air-conditioned. That's a loose description. It was a large room with a kitchen at one end and three massive window-type air conditioners on one wall. The good news was that the units were on the north wall, always in the shade and remarkably efficient though they roared like train engines. The bad news was that with 95° heat, 80% humidity, and the sun beating down on an uninsulated tin roof, only an iceberg planted squarely in the middle of the room could have made the place bearable. It was the thought that counted.

We always started our shows with some upbeat silliness, stole some tunes from the Andrew Sisters, or the English Lark, Jane Froman, did a little rock, a little Broadway, and closed with some sappy thing from the Everly Brothers. The lead moved from woman to woman whether there were four of us or twelve of us performing. The medley took approximately 25 minutes to work through, then we would salute the birthday boy or boys, take a few requests, and be packing our gear 45 minutes after we walked through the door.

That day a tall, thin young man in a wheelchair requested, *The First Time*. Sarah started the keyboard intro as I strolled across the room.

About ten feet from the wheelchair, I realized that the GI had well-bandaged stumps where his hands had been.

"Hi, soldier," I said. "Looks like you had a bad day."

He nodded. "Yes, Ma'am. Bad fuse. Shell blew up in my hands."

As he looked toward me, I realized that he was focusing on the place where the sound of my voice had been, not where I was standing now, three feet in front of him. He had lost his vision as well as his hands.

I swallowed hard and felt the tears begin to swell.

"I'm going to walk around behind you and put my arms around your neck, if that's okay with you, sort of like I was your girl back home."

He grinned and nodded.

"Then I'm going to sing to you. It's okay if the other guys listen, isn't it?"

"Yes, Ma'am." He smiled in my direction.

I walked behind him, put my arms around his neck.

Then I sang – and cried. And I've never sung that song again.

Sometimes by Alys Caviness-Gober
(a 2018 *NICE* entry; inspired by *The Brothers Karamazov*)

> I hear the Witching Hour approach
> saturated with dark reproach
> when yesterday's undaunted path
> became Destiny's rigid wrath;
>
> sometimes I yearn to tread once more
> my footsteps backwards through that door,
> sometimes I yearn once more to see
> a path unspoken awaiting me.

As Autumn Falls by Alys Caviness-Gober

So Far, So Good by Steve VandeWater
(*song lyric*)

You know the wife she made me start upon a diet t'other day.
To keep me young and healthy is her plan.
But it's goin' mighty poorly and I really gotta say
That rabbit food don't satisfy a full-grown man.

Well now my plate looks like a Chia Pet all covered up with sprouts,
And quinoa really puts me off my feed.
Tell me what the hell is "gluten free" and tofu all about?
And ain't no way I'm EVER eatin' raw sea weed!

Well they tell me dyin' early sure would be an awful shame,
But in spite of eatin' crap so long, I'm healthy just the same.
So I'm fallin' off the wagon, eatin' things I never should.
No I may not live forever but so far, so good.
Instrumental Break

Well in the news you see folks livin' to 100 years or more.
And reporters ask 'em how they lived so long.
"Eggs and bacon ev'ry morning,' grits and taters by the score"
Is what keeps 'em feelin' chipper, so it can't be wrong.

I think that drinkin' filtered water, and that bland unsweetened tea
Is nasty but it's healthy so they say.
But then beer is healthy too my friend, and tastes real good to me
So I reckon that I'll drink it 'til my final day.

There ain't none of us immortal, no we'll never get that wish
So I'll keep on eatin' like a horse, and drinkin' like a fish
Why you'd wanna live forever, I've just never understood
Guess I'll hang on 'til I kick it then, so far, so good.

I wouldn't wanna live forever, even if they said I could
So I'm just livin' for today. So far, so good.

Second Thoughts by Nancy Simmonds
(a 2018 *NICE* entry, inspired by *Follow the River*)

Racing along the deer track
distracted
by what she thought she heard

was it the faint cry of alarm?
an infant's mewl?
a bellow of anger?

she trips over the exposed root
landing hard on wrist and hip.

This cry is hers.

In the after silence
a hair-thin voice
teases the night.

An owl replies.
Bats take wing.

The river roars on
rushing fast and past
her torn skirts
her bloody lip
the frayed ropes dragging in the mud.

A fallen tree hugs the shore
a driftwood train to freedom.

That lonely sound on the wind beckons
pulling her backwards.

She chews a broken fingernail.

Has her life completely unraveled?
Can her decision be undone?

Behind Another Door by Alys Caviness-Gober

Back in the Good Old Days by Mary Couch

Oh if only, we could slide backward in time
to those olden days when coke was a dime.
Where fins were the latest style on each car,
and we'd catch lightning bugs in a mason jar.

We'd spend weekends with picnics in the park,
and no one feared going out after dark.
Our music came on black vinyl not CD,
and we spent evenings with a book to read.

On summer days, we loved an ice cream bar
while at the drive-in movies in our car.
Every clerk would count change at the store,
and milk was delivered to our front door.

We'd play hide and seek in our yard outside,
and on Sundays we'd all go for a ride.
Then play checkers, baseball, or kick the can,
and our air conditioning was an old box fan.

Life was less stressful, a slower pace and age,
then the world evolved, turned another page.
Now technology has come to change our ways.
Yet we recall with fondness those olden days.

Echo of the Ancient Ones by Marlene Million
(a 2018 *NICE* entry, inspired by *Follow the River*)

*"Sometimes I cry by the great
beauty of it all. Ordinary things
become extraordinary."*
– Fool's Crow

Formations on the wall of the cave
intertwine like lives in time.
Manifestations, divine revelations
of eternal truth emerge from motionless stone.

You, the Chief, stand solemn and tall
in the midst of your people, arms crossed,
your wife at your side, with child.

Within the darkness of the cave, you deliver
to all who may witness the illumination
of your beliefs and hopes. Between the layers
of time are written the laws within your heart.
Wisdom seeps forth like moisture from the rocks.

I have journeyed here to commune with nature,
to ponder Mother Earth. Many hikers
pass this hallowed ground oblivious
to your presence, a people, proud and strong.

I sit upon this ancient stone, surrounded by the people
of your nation. Drums echo the heartbeat
of the universe – this moment reverberates deep
within my spirit and within my life.

Lily Top by W.B. Cornwell

As the buggy pulled into the drive and the carriage halted, the door was opened by a man I had never seen before. He was young, about twenty or so, and of regular appearance. Father stepped out and lent his hand to Mother, helping her out of the buggy. I hadn't been to Mother's childhood home, which was called Lily Top, since the one time when I was a very young lad of five or so, even though at fifteen I was still looked at as young by most. Mother's family was a wealthy old family whose roots seemed older than America itself. Most of her family were terribly displeased when she married Father, who was considered nouveau-riche. Father owned a successful line of department stores that boomed soon after the Civil War. He was twenty-four and Mother was only seventeen when they ran off to marry in the secret of night.

Lily Top was grand home with a somewhat ominous feel about it as it was draped in snow and icicles hung from the ornate roof, making the house look like it had teeth and was just waiting to eat us all alive. This winter-cursed quasi-castle was nothing like I remembered it from my five-year-old perspective, then it was a summer dream, and the landscape reflected the name, hills as far as the eye could see all covered in wild lilies. You would imagine that I would have been afraid of a mere house at five, not fifteen. It is funny how things sometimes happen.

Little did I know that after this visit I would never be the same. We talked into the foyer, and we gave our coats, hats, gloves, and scarves to the maid who swiftly took them away.

Mother took Father's hand, "Isaac, thank you for bringing me here."

He looked at her with such love. "Just remember, I didn't do it because it was asked of me from your mother, but because you asked me to." He leaned in to kiss her when a man cleared his throat, interrupting them.

"Please make your way to the parlor, Miss Amanda," the man said. "Your family is waiting."

Mother sighed, "It's Mrs. Arasmith. Mrs. Isaac Arasmith."

She then walked into the doorway on the right. Father and I followed. I was taken aback by the beauty of the inside of the house. I couldn't clearly remember what it looked like before, but seeing it again filled my mind with the forgotten splendor. The walls were deep-rich mahogany. The floor a rose-hued marble that surrounded the islands of oriental rugs, upon which was exquisite furniture, inhabited by people I assumed were relatives. They wore an array of beautiful clothing and jewels, living up to the elegant expectations that came along with their breeding. Mother was dressed much more simply, yet far more the epitome of a lady. She could have walked in wearing all of the diamonds, emeralds, rubies, and pearls that Father spoiled her with, but this meeting to her was not a social gathering. She had come to say goodbye to her mother.

One of the women stood, "Amanda, you've come."

She was a larger woman with dark hair like Mother's and the same blue eyes. She walked over to Mother and hugged her. Mother barely put her arms around her in return.

"Hello, Anna." Mother said as they parted.

Mother looked around, starting with a woman that was tall and thin; she, too had dark hair and blue eyes.

"Amanda." the woman nodded.

"Julia," Mother replied.

Father whispered to me, "Those are your mother's older sisters."

A man who I believed could have been my grandfather was seated next to my Aunt Julia, he spoke causing his handlebar mustache to shake like a caterpillar on the run, "Amanda, I say, is that your boy?"

Mother turned and smiled, "Yes. Ezra, I want you to meet your family." After pointing out the aunts again, she told me that the old man, Albert, was, in fact, Aunt Julia's husband. She pointed to another man who was of a more appropriate age and told me that he was Aunt Anna's husband, Leonard. She then directed my attention to the most beautiful girl I had ever seen, and said, "this must be Alexandra."

"How do you do?" the blonde-haired angel asked.

"How do you do?" I was nervous to respond.

"Alexandra is your cousin." Mother smiled.

"I see." I tried to hide that the fact I was enamored with her.

"Alex," Aunt Julia spoke, "take Ezra to the kitchen and have Cook give you both some cake, we have family matters to talk about, and you two are not needed."

Alexandra walked over to me, and I felt goose bumps form across my body as she took my hand. "Come with me." She smiled, and I felt as though I would make an utter spectacle of myself if anyone were to notice the sweat that was beginning to form on my brow.

Once in the kitchen, the cook gave us the cake that Alexandra told her that we were sent for and then we sat at the small uncovered wooden table and ate off of China that, once cleared, showed an "M" in the center. The "M" stood for Marshall, which was mother's name before marriage. Alexandra slowly removed the fork from her plump lips and asked, "Are you sad that our grandmother is dying?"

I didn't know what to say. I picked up my napkin and used it to remove any crumbs or smudges of frosting from my face. "I can't say that I am. I don't know her. I am sorry for all of the family, however."

She smiled. "Well, the world won't miss her very much. Besides, all of her daughters want her dead. They will each inherit a small fortune."

I was shocked and then angry. "My mother is a good person. I can't speak for yours, but my mother would never want to see someone die just for money."

She looked down for a second before standing and walking to me. "My mother is not your Aunt Julia. Ezra, I am not a Marshall. Julia is my step-mother. My real mother died when I was born."

I stood and looked into her bright green eyes. "I'm very sorry. I didn't know."
"It's quite alright. After all, since we aren't really family, that means that this is perfectly fine to do." She wrapped her arms around me and kissed me. It was my first kiss, and it was thrilling. She was so perfect and the moment was truly magical. After a few moments we parted, and she looked at me smiling and said, "Very nice." Before I could say anything, and my skin must have still been flushed, the maid walked in and told me that my grandmother, Mrs. Marshall, had requested to see me.

Mother walked me up the stairs and down a long hall with walls covered in paintings of my ancestors. We came to the end of the hall and stood before a large set of double doors that were engraved with excellent craftsmanship.

Mother took my face in her hands. "Ezra, please be on your best behavior. Your grandmother is very ill, and she asked to see you, to see how I've done as your mother. Show her what a fine young man you are."

She then ran her hand through my hair to fix a few of the loose stands. Mother opened the doors and made way for me. I looked into the spacious room that was all cream on cream, lace, and swooping layers of silk at the windows and framing the walls. It was like an elaborate cake in the window of a French baker. As I walked in, I heard the doors creak behind me, as they were closed slowly, a sign of how nervous Mother was.

"Ezra Arasmith," a voice called out, "come here."

I looked at the bed and saw a small woman with elegant features. She looked like my mother but thirty years older. Her head was covered with a cap, and yet I could see a little of her dark hair as I got closer. Her eyes were also the same blue as Mother's and my aunts.'

"Take a seat," she pointed to a chair that sat by the bed. She sat up straighter and cleared her throat. "Now, tell me, Ezra Arasmith, what do you think of Lily Top?"

I was nervous, and I wanted to appear to be well-versed in social graces, yet as I opened my mouth to reply my voice cracked and I had to clear my throat and try again.

"I find it to be a magnificent home, Grandmother."

She let out a little sigh. "What is it that you want to do?"

"I beg your pardon?"

"For your trade, what will you do once you are a man?"

"Oh, I - I, would like to take over my father's business."

"Hmm." she said, "Pour me a drink."

She pointed to her bedside table where there was a glass and a pitcher. I stood and walked to the table. I started to pour the water as I shifted my eyes over to her to see her watching me.

Once the glass was half full, she held up her hand, "That will be enough."

I put the pitcher down and picked up the glass and brought it to her.

She took a long and slow drink. She then handed it back to me. I sat it back on the table and returned to my seat. I looked at her and she at me.

"That will be all," she said, waving me toward the doors.

I stood there for a moment, unsure of what she thought and what would happen. I looked to Mother as she walked toward me, her hands folded. She was still nervous and white as a ghost. She tried to smile, but couldn't force enough happiness to convince her lips to turn up fully.

"Mama," I said, "she was done talking to me. I just hope that I made you proud." She pulled me into her arms and pressed her to cheek to my head.

Soon Mother, her sisters, and Alexandra all went to sleep. My father and my two uncles all stayed up to smoke cigars and drink some brandy from crystal glasses that belonged to my grandfather, a fact that I was unaware of until Uncle Leonard brought it up with the side note of how much he would like to have them after Grandmother died.

"Oh, they are nice," Father said as he swirled the liquor in his glass again, "but, do you think that Phoebe would want you to have them?" I had never known what Grandmother's first name was until then.

"How do you mean?" Leonard asked in a huff.

"Phoebe has never liked you," Father said as a matter-of-factly. He then took another drag from his cigar.

"Let me tell you what for, Isaac Arasmith!" Leonard stood and waved his glass around spilling drops of his drink. "You know how much Ignatius and Phoebe opposed Amanda marrying you. Don't think they've ever cared about you!"

"I'm not pretending that they did, or that Phoebe will even have a change of heart before she joins Old Ignatius. I find it humorous how much they never liked you."

"Why?" Leonard shouted, "They hated you, too!"

"Yes," Father said as he took another drink, "they never got to know me. You, on the other hand, they knew very well and for many years, and they still hated you."

Just then Albert began to burst out with laughter, "Good point, Ike, good point!"

Leonard looked at Albert and shouted, "You be quiet, old man."

Albert hammered his cane on the floor, causing the marble to reply with a sharp scream. "Who are you calling old?"

"I'm speaking to you, Methuselah!" Leonard bellowed.

"Now, now," Father interrupted, "calm down. We are all here for our wives as they come to terms with saying goodbye to their dear mother. No need to quarrel amongst ourselves."

"Agreed," Albert said.

Leonard took a deep breath, and his face went from red back to his normal shade, and he sat back down. I looked to my father amazed at his skill to start a fight and say all of the things he wished to and also be the peacemaker. We all sat there for a moment when the butler came in to stir the fire. I watched the embers as they danced in the fireplace.

Father nudged me with his elbow, and he held his glass to me. "Son, would you like to try it?"

I was nervous, as I heard that it burns. But to be brave and to act like the man that I wanted to be – the man in front of me – I took the glass and quickly took a drink. My mouth filled with that liquid blaze of caramel-colored fire. Father took the nearly empty cup from my hand, and I gasped as I inhaled the cool air and it met the heat from the brandy in the center of my throat. I feared a tornado would be born. I started to cough, and Father whacked my back trying to help. After a minute I was fine, aside from my bruised ego. I excused myself to go to sleep.

In the morning, we all gathered around the large dining table for breakfast. Mother was barely eating. I wished that I would be able to help her, but there was nothing I could do. Her mother, a mother that she had not talked to in years, was dying. After the meal was over, I went for a walk around the grounds. The snow was falling lightly, my coat, thick woolen gloves, and scarf kept me warm as I strolled in the slumbering garden. The marble statues and birdbaths were encased in a glazing of crystal-like ice and topped with mounds of snow. I stood in the center of three trees and looked up to the large branches that were bare and gnarled like a witch's hand reaching out to the other trees as if the coven was about to join hands. I heard an echo of a creaking sound. I turned to see the back of a young woman sitting on a swing that hung from one of the trees. I could tell by her long hair and petite frame that it was Alexandra.

I walked over to her and said, "Would you like me to push you so you can go higher?"

She stopped by pressing her feet through the snow to the frozen earth and turned to me. "I want to fly." she said with a twinkle in her eye.

I stood behind her and inhaled the scent of roses that wafted from her. I pushed and pushed she went higher and higher and still.

She shouted, "Higher Ezra! Higher!"

The snow from the branches fell upon us, dusting us like sugar. After a while, my arms got tired, and slowly the swing began to not go as high. Finally, I took hold of the rope and stopped it all together.

She stood and shook the snow from her person and looked at all of the snow that had fallen on me and laughed. She started to brush the snow off of my coat, and I again felt tingles as her hands touched my body. She placed her hands on my shoulders, and this time she left them in place and looked me in the eyes for a long moment. I raised my hands to her face, my gloved hands nervous to touch her rosy cheeks. I pulled her into me, and this time I kissed her. It was a rush, but different than before. I held her close, and she broke the kiss only to begin kissing my cheeks and chin and forehead and then my lips again. She then stepped out of my arms. "Someone is calling us."

As my heart started to return to its normal rate and the daze, or sensation of young love, began to wear off, I heard my father's voice, "Ezra. Alexandra. Come inside."

We rushed to the house, trying not to trip in the snow. We ran inside, shook the snow off of our things and entered the living room. I saw Mother, Father, my aunts and uncles and an old man I'd never seen before. My mother and her sisters were all three crying with lace-trimmed hankies held to either their puffy eyes or running noses. Alexandra looked to me as if she could read my mind. My grandmother had died.

"Son," Father stood and walked me to the old man, "this is Mr. Kalahar, your late grandfather's dear friend and lawyer. This is Ezra."

He looked at me, his round frame glasses needing to be pushed up the bridge of his nose to see me clearly.

"Master Arasmith." He began grabbing at his papers that were scattered across the table before him. "I have a few things for you to sign. Of, course, your father will need to sign as well since you are still under age."

"What are Ezra and Isaac signing for?" asked Uncle Leonard.

"Ezra's inheritance," replied Mr. Kalahar.

"Ezra's?" Leonard stood, "That child should only be getting what is coming to Amanda."

"Well, Phoebe disagreed," said Mr. Kalahar, "all three of her and Ignatius' daughters will receive a few things, but the bulk of the estate is going to Ezra."

I couldn't believe it. Everything was mine. But why? I couldn't understand it. I was trying to sort through my feelings. After a time, I remembered my surroundings and the fighting brought me back to reality.

"It's not fair!" yelled Uncle Leonard.

"Relax, Leonard," said Aunt Anna. "We have enough."

"Your mother was the wealthiest person in this county. Everything should be split between you and Anna. Your parents disowned Amanda, and now her child, a child born out of disgrace, is getting everything!"

"I will not stand for you talking about my son like that!" Father said.

"Stop it, just stop it!" said Aunt Julia as she stood and threw her china cup and saucer to the floor. "Leonard, you are an evil, vile man. Our mother is dead!" She ran from the room crying. Mother followed after her sister, calling out for her to come back.

"If you can all conduct yourselves for a short period of time I can read to you all the details of the will." said Mr. Kalahar.

Uncle Leonard sat with a huff. Mr. Kalahar looked to Father and me. "Will you please be seated?" Father sat and motioned for me to as well. "Now, let's begin."

The will went on to state that Aunt Anna was left a collection of ivory animal figurines, grandmother's silver dressing table set, three William and Mary chairs that belonged to grandfather's parents, a pearl necklace, a ruby broach, a pair of diamond earrings, a gold hair comb, and a cameo and pearl bracelet. Aunt Julia was left a set of silver candle holders, a jade figurine of a geisha that stood nearly two feet tall, a collection of leather-bound books that belonged to Grandfather, Grandmother's topaz suit, a diamond ring, a pair of ruby earrings, and a gold and diamond tiara. Alexandra was left a cameo brooch and pair of pearl earrings. A lace tablecloth was to be sent to Mother's cousin in Philadelphia, and a silver tea service was left to another one of Mother's cousins in Atlanta.

Everything else was mine.

Once the reading was over, Uncle Leonard stormed off after repeatedly saying that he would not be attending the funeral. Aunt Anna followed him. Alexandra and I kept glancing at each other. Father's voice took my attention away from her.

He asked Mr. Kalahar, "There is nothing for Amanda?"

Mr. Kalahar put his hand into his monogrammed leather bag and pulled out an envelope, "There is this." He handed it to Father, across it was written, *Amanda*. Father stood, "I'll take it to her at once."

"May I?" I jumped to my feet.

Father looked at me for a moment and nodded, handing me the envelope.

I went to the doorway of the room my parents were staying in and knocked on the door.

"Come in," Mother said.

"Mother, I have something for you from Mr. Kalahar."

She was packing her things. Pausing, she crossed the room and sat on the bed, patting on the quilt next to her. I handed her the envelope as I sat down.

"This is Mother's handwriting," she said with a sigh before opening it, and she read aloud,

My dearest Amanda,
I hope that you never felt unloved. There are many times I regret letting you go and not keeping in touch more. Your father was a proud man, too proud at times. I know that he loved you, too, but it was too hard for him to accept that you married Isaac against his wishes. As you know by now, there was nothing left to you in the will that your father wrote for me, and I could not change a word. I was, however, able to talk him into leaving everything to Ezra, his only grandchild. I know that Ezra will give you anything that you want, and you will be taken care of. I know you may not see it as I do, but in

a way, I am leaving everything to you, in hopes that you will forgive me for all of the wrongs that I have done.
With love, Mother

Mother began to weep and laid her head on my shoulder. "Why didn't she tell me? Why?"

After a moment she spoke again. "Our last talk was about trivial things. She could have told me! If I would have known how she really felt I would have wrapped my arms around her and kissed her and told her that I loved her and that I always did. I loved my mother, Ezra, I did."

As she cried again, I held her close.

Inheriting Lily Top was like inheriting a kingdom. The King and Queen were gone, and I was now sitting on the throne, but what good is a throne built of heartache? What good is a castle built of pain?

Home by Alys Caviness-Gober
(a 2018 *NICE* entry; inspired by *The Odyssey*)

When the sea grass whispers my name
through leeward winds,
and the indigo stained sky shines down
into caressing waves,
and the great-tailed grackle steps so lightly
across hot diamond sands,
then, yes, and only then
will I again breath in
the sweet southern salty air
of home.

Renn by Bryony Stanger

Revenge on the Grumpy Old Man by Steve VandeWater

There's a guy who lives just a few houses from me
I call him the Grumpy Old Man.
He's always come off as a bit of a jerk
I avoid him whenever I can.
He's the kind of a guy who is fussy as Hell
'Bout his house and his car and his grass.
He's retired and has nothing better to do
Than to be the neighborhood ass.

In the Summertime, standing there shaking his fist
He warns kids, "Stay off of my lawn."
In October when Trick or Treat rolls around
Though he's home, he pretends that he's gone.

In short, he's unfriendly, a pain in the butt
With disdain for both neighbors and pets.
But if that's the way he intends to be,
Then I guess he'll just get what he gets.

I've been thinking of ways to get under his skin
And believe I've come up with a plan.
In my basement I have a grow light you see
And come Springtime he'll be a sad man.

I'm growing some dandelions. Thousands of them!
When they ripen to fuzzy white weeds
I'll take out my Remington razor and then
I'll shave them clean down to the seeds.

Then on some dark night when the weather is warm
Sometime between midnight and dawn
I'll take out my harvested dandelion seeds
and I'll spread them all over his lawn.

Obey All Traffic Laws by Jess Coovert

It was sunny that day, in the old part of town
As I drove down the road with my father sat
In the passenger seat of our 1984 Buick in this
Hideous blue color my father and I hated but
Mother enjoyed it so we kept the paint that way,
Chipped as it was.

Turn left up here.

We were cruising down the road
At a steady twenty five miles per hour
As houses, some new and some decaying,
Passed by the window and my mind started
To wander to the families that resided inside
Each home when lights flickered to life
In windows behind curtains.

Watch the road, watch the road.

I hit the lever to the left of the steering wheel,
The left-hand turn signal blinking and clicking –
Tick tick tick tick tick tick tick tick tick tick –
While I sat motionless at a stop sign for a moment
Too long and the car behind us honked before
Swerving around us and my father said,
"Turn left, son, you need to turn left. It's your turn."

Brake. Brake. Brakebrakebrake. That was a squirrel.

Logan Street came into view with its worn
Brick surface and small houses that seemed
So big all those years ago when I was the same age
As my daughter, who is sitting in the driver's seat
This time with her hands clenched around the wheel
And knuckles white as she stares at the rocky expanse
Of possibility stretched ahead of her.

Weeds Along The River by Alys Caviness-Gober

Where There Was a River by Jerry Dreesen
(a 2018 *NICE* entry, inspired by *Follow the River*)

Loving Spirits

Our spirits mingle in
love like the clear
swirling waters of the
mountain stream
~ Red Bear

There is no river here,
only an arrogant
reservoir that once was a river

before it ate the tall grass
drowned the willows, swallowed villages,
and the fields of corn that fed them.

It was a river of quiet passage,
canoes without sound going and coming.
silent except for the sawing of crickets.

hawks hovering high over the fields
where at night one could hear the river
flow and the tree frogs sing in search for a mate.

There is no river here, no smooth river rocks,
where crayfish flourished and children watched
the evening stars from under a willow tree.

There is no river. The corn and
canoes are gone, the tree frogs and
crickets, the tall grass that hid young lovers.

Only echoes of the river are
left, its gentle voice, the silent,
slow roll to the distant, inevitable sea.

Quiverfull by Leslie Ober

Looking Back ~ A Story of Redemption by Leslie Ober

If someone would have told me twelve years ago that I would have half a dozen kids one day, I would have laughed in their face. I was young, married, and desperate to be with child. Yet my body betrayed me again and again. We had been happily married for a few years when we got the surprise of a lifetime. Two pink lines slowly emerged within the window of that plastic test.

We were pregnant. I was overwhelmed with excitement and instantly began dreaming and planning.

However, two months into the pregnancy, everything came to a screeching halt. After a dramatic trip to the ER, we discovered that the baby no longer had a heartbeat. My body was in the midst of miscarrying our dead baby, and my heart broke into a million little pieces. It took a LONG time to pick myself back up from that loss.

Years later, we decided that we were ready and that it was time to try again. After a few months of trying to conceive, we were both cautiously excited to be pregnant again. However, the excitement was short-lived as we experienced the same, abrupt ending two months into it. There are no words that I can even put into place on this page that would describe the utter anguish my heart endured through that second loss.

"What is wrong with me that I can't even do the ONE thing I am supposed to be able to do?" I implored. "I HATE my body." "What if I will never be able to have children?" "Perhaps this just isn't meant to be," I reasoned. I begged God to take away my desire. Why did I even want to have a child? Couldn't I be fine with it just being the two of us? We got a new puppy after that loss and decided to enjoy her as we sorted through our grief.

I ended up needing a surgery to help treat endometriosis – a condition known to cause infertility. After the surgery and getting the go-ahead from the OBGYN, we made the heart-wrenching decision to try to conceive once again. Month after month passed, and my mind began playing tricks on me. I felt foolish for thinking that this could actually happen. So I slowly shut down the idea of being a mom. I told myself that I was fine and didn't really want to have kids anyway.

But then, I heard God speak. It wasn't a loud, booming voice. But rather, a soft, whisper within my heart and mind. I heard Him say, *"Trust Me. Do not be afraid to ask Me for exactly what you want. Don't stop asking."*

So from that day forward, I allowed myself to hope again. I prayed and asked God to be with child again. I asked for a healthy baby. I allowed myself to feel once again. It was so incredibly difficult. But I kept on – every single day. I hoped. I asked. I believed. And at the end of that month of being on my knees before God, I was given what I had asked for. Those two pink lines once again appeared before my eyes . . . eyes that filled with tears – of joy and a little bit of fear. We were pregnant, and this time everything felt different.

And it was. With a fairly easy pregnancy, I carried our firstborn, a son, to full term. After the difficulties we had had prior to having our son, we chose not to prevent any future pregnancies. And to our surprise, we became pregnant again when he was just seven months old! We welcomed a beautiful daughter exactly 16 months after having our son.

Many couples would have just stopped there. But our hearts were exploding with love for these two miracles and we sensed that our family was not complete. So we continued this journey of building our family and became pregnant again. Sadly, this pregnancy ended quite early with a molar pregnancy, which can become a malignancy.

Thankfully, it had not spread. But we were instructed to not get pregnant for an entire year. So we began preventing. However, in an odd twist of events, while trying to prevent ourselves from getting pregnant, we somehow conceived. We were scared, yet tickled at how this could even have happened. The pregnancy devastatingly ended in yet another miscarriage.

I wrote this at the time:

Dead
But I smile
Anguished
But I'm here
Empty
But I'm searching
God I want you near
A promise broken
My heart is sick
Loved and lost
Again and again
My body betrays me
This world of pain
As I dance with darkness
As I soak in the rain
Pity and Shame
Try to comfort me again
I resist their lies

And reach for anything

Closer to truth
But the truth hurts
And so I am frozen
In the agony
Of my silent struggle
To survive.

We were at a loss for what to do next. Doctors mentioned genetic testing. I grew weary and frustrated with my inability to carry a child within my womb. But we waited until we had the green light to try again. We continued to hope. We prayed like crazy. I remembered that still small voice: *"Trust Me,"* He whispered again.

This journey has a happy ending far greater than anything I could have imagined. We went on to have FOUR more beautiful children, redeeming the four losses we had endured. We have since discovered that some of our kiddos do have mild genetic conditions. And had we chosen to have the genetic testing done after our first two kids, it would be highly likely that we would have been strongly encouraged to stop there. So our choice to forego the testing led to us being blessed beyond measure.

Some may look at our family and think we are crazy (which wouldn't be entirely untrue). Many look at all of our kids and assume that this journey has been easy for us. But if they could only peek into our story, they'd see that it is one full of twists and turns; a journey riddled with impossibly deep heartache, waiting, and trusting in God.

One simple choice: It was the difference between us being a family of four and a family of eight! I hold tight to the verse in the Bible that states: *"Delight yourself in the Lord and He will give you the desires of your heart,"* Psalm 37:4. He asked me to Trust Him. I did. And that has made all the difference. If anyone would have told me all those years ago that I would have the most amazing group of six beautiful children one day, I would not have believed them. Even today, I sometimes have to pinch myself as I wonder, *What did I do to deserve all of these blessings?*

This Memoir by Deborah Petersen

My story has to have a lesson
or it's just a bag of verbs

It has to have smells
and music and silence and
tastes;
It has to have a dance
and visions and
tingling muscle exertion.

My story has to have a lesson
for it's just not mine alone.
It is everyone's story;
It is everyone's verbs.

When this realization came
The Universal
Ah-Ha resounded.

Joey Walnuts' Demise by Kitty O'Doherty

Nature, at its most primal, struck today in my backyard. I'm afraid we
may have lost neighborhood squirrel, Joey Walnuts, to a Red-tailed
Hawk. I was taking my trash to the bin when I noticed a huge hawk
settle in one of the backyard trees. It sat for a minute, then moved to
another tree, and then another. I stared upward and tried to remember
what in Native American belief the sudden appearance of a hawk
represents.

What the sudden appearance of a hawk meant to me became clear:
I had interrupted his attack of what I feared was the entertaining little
rodent I'd fed and watched for the past two years. For there, in the
grass, lay the mortally wounded little guy just a couple of feet from
where I stood.

My neighbor Dave had been in his yard and seen the whole event unfold just before I stepped outside.

"Don't worry," Dave said. "Go back inside, the hawk will come get it."

But it didn't. For an hour, all I could do was watch through the window at what might possibly be the lifeless body of my most favorite squirrel.

I thought about asking Dave to come take the squirrel, but then I got a better idea. I'd do it myself. It was the least I could do to pay my respects to the squirrel who amused me and annoyed my cats. I'd take him somewhere else, someplace scenic and solemn. Someplace by the river where nature could complete its cycle away from my yard. I put on my garden gloves and got some newspaper and a grocery bag. I was kneeling down, rolling the little guy up in the newspaper, and was about to stick him in the grocery bag, when I heard a cheery, "Hello!" behind me. It was my elderly neighbor's sweet daughter Pam, up from Florida visiting the family for the Thanksgiving weekend.

Y'know, it's kind of hard to look normal when you stand up holding a rolled-up newspaper with a squirrel tail sticking out of it. There really was no way to fake anything, so I gave a stuttering explanation while I quickly stuffed the squirrel in the bag. Poor woman probably thought I was bent down planting flower bulbs or something. Yes, I'm your parents' neighbor, I'm so sorry.

But Pam was not outwardly horrified and we had a good laugh. I told her I was about to take the squirrel down by the river and she promised to be a witness for me in case I was arrested for suspicious activity. I appreciated that.

So in the car we went, me and my dead squirrel. I parked in the city lot close to the White River Riverwalk. With bag-o-squirrel in hand, I walked down the path near the old Riverside cemetery; I had a place in mind southward on the path, a semi-secluded brushy area on a high bank above the river. When I got there, a couple of people were hanging out; I decided to turn around. They looked kind of suspicious, but that's a judgment coming from someone who was taking a Sunday walk with a deceased squirrel in a Kroger bag. I headed the other way, wanting to find a suitable spot as quickly as possible.

In the end, I found a great spot off the path under a tree that bent over the river. I unrolled him out of the newspaper and arranged him on his side onto a bed of crispy autumn leaves so he looked like he was sleeping. Goodbye, little guy.

I won't know for a few more days if this was indeed Joey Walnuts. He had such an attitude. A real alpha squirrel.

I'm hoping that one day this week I'll hear my cat Zeke pawing at the window upstairs where Joey would sit in the upper limbs of the tree outside, mocking and taunting him. If that happens, then it will mean that Joey never left.

It will also mean I am a wacky middle-aged lady who performed a funeral ritual for some anonymous rodent.

Grain Elevator II by Alys Caviness-Gober

Perception Is Not Reality by Leslie Ober

Stained by Jenny Kalahar

Stained glass used to frighten me.
It had captured Jesus on the cross
had captured delicate or massive flowers
using the rays of the sun to let us see through
let us stand where colors projected
onto our dress shirts and shoes
onto the rug and pews every Sunday
Never shifting
Never resting

Compressed
Jesus looked miserable.
Nails through His palms suspended Him endlessly
those red flowers and white doves never faded.
Brighter on sunny days
more like rippled plastic when clouds huddled behind

There were so many things to fear:
beauty and flesh pushed flat
bordered in leaded outlines
that would not be picked off
by my tiny fingernails
nor rubbed away by my thumbs

I wanted to rescue Jesus
pull free the nails and lower Him
to the grass-colored carpeting at my feet.
I wanted to hold Him, comfort Him
to revive Him with prayer
as doves flapped and stretched
and soared to their blue heavens.
I wanted to encircle Him with flowers
that had also been set free to bloom into life
as Jesus might
if I could figure out how
to shatter the glass
without shattering our Lord

I know better now.
I've learned about glass and craft
Soldering, staining, cutting
piecing together to make a whole.
I know the flowers aren't real
they aren't trapped.

That blood and piercing nails are metaphors.
Doves were not flattened.
Their wings were never made for flight.
I have no fear when I stand
in the glory of some past craftsman
bathed in glassine colors
of a small church window
in a nearly-forgotten Midwestern town
that is no longer my own

Tranquility I by Alys Caviness-Gober
(*one in a Triptych series*)

Baby Be Kind by Mama's Homemade
(song lyric; written by Kelli Ray Yates and Kat Wedmore)

Baby, you've gotta be kind
This world can make you lose your mind
And things are gonna get hard sometimes
But goddamn, you've gotta be kind

It's hot in the summer, now in winter too
People won't always agree with you
And that's just something you get used to
But goddamn, there's not enough time

Baby, you're not made of stone
Sometimes you might be on your own
You'll know what's right, it's in your bones
So goddamn, you've gotta be strong

You'll get through
And when you do, you'll see

Streets are busy, always such a crowd
They tell you not to be so proud
To keep your eyes fixed on the ground
But goddamn, don't be one of them

Baby, you know you've got my eyes
Look up and wonder at the sky
Don't be afraid, heart open wide
'Cause goddamn, there's so much to see

You'll get through
And when you do, you'll see
It's not enough
To hope for love you gotta be

Baby, you've gotta be kind
This world can make you lose your mind
And things are gonna get hard sometimes
But goddamn, you've gotta be kind

Tranquility II by Alys Caviness-Gober
(one in a Triptych series)

The B Word by Arlene Barker

Journal entry - September 10, 2001
"I was Bored today . . . need to remember the times of anxiety when my mind could never rest. *One never knows what stresses tomorrow may bring.*"

I never use that *B word* anymore.
After the day I wrote it,
the world changed,
and our eyes could not believe it
even after seeing it
again and again and again. I
dream of a quiet sky.
I never use that *B word* anymore. I
wish that on the day before
I wrote it, the empty hands of time

could have spilled a calming water
on to those whose anger seethed in
their wounded hearts and minds. I
wish for simple healing.

I never use that *B word* anymore,
because since the day I wrote it,
time seems a void filled with two
contenders, each hearing only echoes,
each seeing with one eye shut tight, not
able to fully exist as a whole.
I long for peaceful monotony.

I never use that *B word* anymore,
as now I savor empty space
that hides amidst the chaos,
for embracing mundane moments
that may be filled, or just left empty
and beautifully peaceful.
I pray for uneventful tomorrows.

Life (or Something Like It) by Sandy Stewart

The Beginning

Countless eons ago, a tiny glowing mass of squishy pulp undulated
out of a murky, swamp onto an unknown shore. The mass pulsed and
glowed brighter, enduring the itchy sensation of drying scales, while
wondering (sort of) just what it had gotten itself into. Now what?

Quickly noticing the attention its glow was attracting, it turned itself
inside out and blended seamlessly into the surrounding landscape,
worrying about the decisions now facing it. Swamp or shore? Great!

Now it had a decision to make every day. Life had just become
unbearably complicated. Its shape began to change, and strange things
began to happen – over, and over, and over again.

- It glowed; it was eaten.
- It blended; it was consumed with ennui.
- It glowed; it was beheaded.
- It blended; it lived; it died. No one particularly noticed.
- It glowed; it sparkled; it was burned at stake.
- It sparkled PLENTY; its limbs (which it had developed somewhere along the way) were lashed to young trees that were bent over and staked to the ground. The lucky young trees had their ties cut. The unlucky sparkler was torn asunder, learning that limbs can be both a blessing and a curse.
- It was reborn as a cave creature and remained there until it succumbed to a fever born of dankness.
- It was reborn onto a planet without gravity. It soared!
- It was reborn onto a place with nearly everything, called Earth. Gravity became the least of its problems.

Phase Two

Having become a standard issue human, stuff continued to happen – over, and over, and over again. Good stuff, wonderful stuff, weird stuff, bad stuff, worse stuff, horrendous stuff. But there were rest stops in between the plethora of variations. Sometimes it was a male human; sometimes a female; sometimes both. Other times, it wasn't completely sure.

But there were always wonderful options for color! Even boring old beige could be painted and adorned. No matter which option it selected, each of its selves had adventures. Sometimes the adventures were thrilling! Loves happened. Battles were fought. Things were invented. Experiences were had – often over, and over, and over again.

Then, things began to change a little more each time it began again. Sometimes, the changes were very pleasant; sometimes they were terrifying; sometimes excruciatingly painful; sometimes pathetically boring and bland. But morphic resonance ruled, and modifications continued to slowly occur until finally, it decided to roll all these lifetimes of experience into a grand new adventure! You know, just to see what it all really meant, and what it had, or had not, learned.

Phase Three (of Lumpy Gravy)

Once upon a time a little baby girl was born into a bewildered flock of little red hens. Peculiar, but they all tried to make the best of it. The hens earnestly tried to peck her into shape, and she earnestly tried to grow feathers and lay eggs. Flesh was pummeled; feathers were ruffled; feelings were hurt. Eventually, they all became more tolerant, and agreed to just love each other. Someone shouted (or clucked) *"Vive La Différence!"* Oddly enough, none of them had previously spoken (or clucked) in French. But, miraculously, they all understood.

And that, dear ones, is evolution!

Global Warming will be addressed in a future missive.

Tranquility III by Alys Caviness-Gober
(one in a Triptych series)

For Mary Draper Ingles by Sarah E. Morin
(a 2018 *NICE* entry; inspired by *Follow the River*)

*For Mary Draper Ingles, who was captured in a Shawnee raid in
1755. While working at a salt lick, she took her chance to escape,
leaving behind her newborn.*

Judge my crime; a mother's fault.
Who could abandon her own child?
My hands and cheeks crusted with salt.

My first chance since Shawnee assault
to escape into the wild.
Judge my crime; a mother's fault.

My babe, with skin as pale as malt
has this dark-skinned girl beguiled.
My hands and cheeks crusted with salt.

His cries would bring my journey halt:
this newborn babe, so weak and mild.
Judge my crime; a mother's fault.

A ruined woman by default.
Shall history call me reviled?
My hands and cheeks crusted with salt.

Forgive me, husband, God on alt.
I'll flee, but leave behind my child.
Judge my crime; a mother's fault.
My hands and cheeks crusted with salt.

McGregor Park by Lawrence "Rick" Phillips

On a sunny Sunday afternoon in early Fall 2014 my wife Sheryl and I went to a new park near our home in Central Indiana just north of Indianapolis. MacGregor Park is a rather large park and not well developed at the time. It was our first visit, and we had not prepared for a long hike.

This urban park is vast with many trails it was difficult to know where we were or where we were going. Due to budget restrictions at that time, the trails were not well marked. We walked in a circle and then another. We strolled in a wonderfully primordial thick old growth of Indiana woods where we witnessed the hints of red and orange in the sugar maples and sycamores that filled the dense area. Then we walked into a lush prairie with waist-high and shoulder-high wildflowers, weeds, and grasses. The smell of the flowers and the crops soon to be harvested in a nearby field was intoxicating.

Wooded and grassy areas in Indiana, Ohio, Kentucky, and Illinois are truly fantastic. The grass shimmers as the breeze blows across it and the woods talk in whispers and cracks as the sun first heats then later the air cools the dense mass of cover. The woods offer shade, but it also traps moisture which creates a surreal experience of large trees, downed rotting wood, and dense undergrowth. I grew up playing, hiking, camping, and intentionally getting lost in areas like these, and on that day, I felt right at home. It is no wonder that MacGregor Park brought out the boy in me.

As I walked with Sheryl, I was a young man before I had diabetes or rheumatoid arthritis, exploring woods near Kokomo, and finding the pearls of Indiana as I used to call them. These were secret places where few would go and where I would imagine myself being among the first humans to visit a ravine or see a downed tree. In those days before the disease, it was awesome to be a kid and not worry about apple juice for low blood sugar, my last injection, joints that might stop working, or being so tired I needed to sit down every few feet. When I was not yet 17 and disease was an abstract concept, Indiana was an amazing place to grow up, and this day in McGregor Park I imagined I was a young man standing tall, confident in his abilities and completely at home in this wonderful place.

All was good – perfect even – until my wife's expression turned from joy to worry as we went further on our walk. Sheryl must have sensed my concern as we passed the same tree twice and I realized we were hopelessly lost.

Being lost was a frightening predicament for my otherwise tough and resilient wife. Unlike me, Sheryl never went wandering off for an afternoon in dense woods, with a backpack, compass, and the hope she could find her way out. In the 1960s, boys were encouraged to 'get lost' and find their way home, but girls were not. Sheryl had little experience finding her way around an unfamiliar woods.

There were possible repercussions to our being lost that truly terrified Sheryl. What if I fainted, my knees stopped moving, or I grew too tired to continue. What if my blood sugar plummeted or my feet swelled from using the rough path? Even a cell phone wouldn't be much help. We couldn't tell people where we were. They might not find us in time.

I thought my wife was overreacting and our disagreement resulted in a stalemate, with me wanting to go on, and Sheryl demanding we return the way we had come.

Our little dog, Samantha, sided with my wife, looking bold for the first trip around the grassy area but increasingly timid as my wife's anxiety grew. Samantha had been leading the way, but with every step forward she turned her head as if to gauge our reaction. Samantha always sided with my wife in such matters, and as Sheryl grew more anxious, Samantha grew more timid.

I was not anxious about being lost. On the contrary, for the first time in some time, I felt good. My joints were working, and my hands could squeeze. I loved the air, the feeling of being adrift, and the challenge to find a way out of the woods. I wanted to visit a magic ravine, a new pearl of Indiana, like I did all those summer days ago in my youth. For that moment I did not have diabetes or RA, I was not a patient; I felt alive once more.

However, Samantha and Sheryl won out; the vote was a decisive two to one: find the way back. So, we turned around, retraced our steps, and ended up where we started. When we got back to the car, my blood sugar had dropped a lot, and I did not have apple juice or glucose tabs on our trek. At the car, I was no longer a boy in the woods, but a 57-year-old person with diabetes and RA, whose blood sugar was dropping like a rock with a throbbing hip. Sheryl's safe way got us out of trouble.

On that day (and most days), I had forgotten the lessons of what I have learned so many times over the course of my life with these diseases. Thankfully Sheryl (and Samantha) knew then what I still cannot learn today, that there are limits that my health set. For me, I am still that boy who loves getting lost in the woods just to find his way home, and Sheryl is still that girl who was encouraged to be safe.

(Unfortunately, Samantha lost her many health battles in 2016, but she remains our companion in our life journey.)

A Cautionary Tale of an Evil Carbohydrate by Crystal Morrison

Captain Yukon saw the familiar sign as he crested the hill.
His journey home near complete, only 10 miles from Spudsville.
He had an ominous feeling when he turned down the lane
and noticed an additional sign reading, "Where Insanity Reigns."

"Abandon all hope!" warned a makeshift sign at the border.
Smirking he thought, "Should I be afraid of shells and mortar?"
Nothing could dissuade this spud of noble birth
for he was a Russet, and his roots ran deep in this earth.

Not long after arriving, his bravado subsided.
"You'll learn who's in control," the weary townsfolk chided.
To his horror he discovered the insane Potato Queen
with her blood red lips and eyes with a baleful gleam.

She controlled everyone from her royal plantation,
and decided their fates without hesitation.
The wicked Queen Julienne was the Chief Justice and Supreme Spud.
She could make you cream of the crop, or leave you face-down in the mud.

She had absolute authority and ruled with an iron fist.
Many potatoes went to ground, lest they make her hit list.
Woe be the spud found guilty of a crime.
Would he be boiled, diced, mashed, or fried?

Had Captain Yukon only heeded that first warning sign,
he'd not have been conscripted into her army for all time.
Now he found himself a guard in her regimental bin,
quelling the town's fears as she screeched, "Off with their skins!"

Crisalys Poetry Collage by Alys & Cris Gober
(the latter participated rather unwillingly)

Scarlet Letter by Zoe VandeWater

(song lyric)

A scarlet letter
Attached to you,
An act of sin
You swore you didn't do.

Just be honest babe
Who'd you lie with in my bed?
Hurry up now,
You're covered in red.

So go ahead and plead your case to me
You're here because of your own greed.
So I don't feel bad for what I gotta do
The deed is done, now my heart's in two.

A pretty lie,
Or maybe more,
Have led to me
Knockin' down this door.

Just be honest babe,
I caught you in the act.
Now I'm wonderin'
Who's knife's in who's back?

So go ahead and plead your case to me
You're here because of your own greed.
So I don't feel bad for what I gotta do
The deed is done, now my heart's in two.

You had your chance
To become a better man.
Now here we stand,
You with a girl and me with blood on my hands.

It's too late to plead your case to me
You're here because of your own greed.
So I don't feel bad for what I had to do
The deed is done, now my heart's in two.

Gone by Alys Caviness-Gober

Rolling By by Jenny Kalahar

I remember
we remember
you remember crawling across a dew-dripped lawn
watching straight, sparkling blades of bright grass
desperately try to shake themselves free of dandelions
calling for help from careless, clouded winds
until those moist, yellow heads turned puff dry and gray
and finally did blow away
giving up
or giving in to the magic

I remember
we remember
you remember walking the carpeted aisle of a train
passing seated and overheated travelers
half-asleep in the dullness
of rumbling past everything.
You stopped at a vacant seat
knelt to stare through a grimy window

and the train stopped to expel you
into a field of summer's rusty wheat
depositing you like its egg in a farmyard.
You hatched and grew to become
another train yourself
loaded up with humanity
your travelers half-asleep in the jostling stuffiness
bored with the world rolling by your new, clean windows
and missing everything, everything
every mile of wild, fantastic magic rolling by

We know better now
and have learned our lessons:
that carrying passengers on any ride is dangerous
and heartbreaking
but it seems to be the purpose of hatching in farmyards
why we've cracked through a fleshy shell
bits of it still clinging into adulthood
carrying others along who are disinterested
unaware that we are blowing them to where they must be
with help from careless, clouded winds of chance and design
loving or hating our dandelions
until we are puff dry and gray
and finally do blow away
giving up
or giving in to the magic

Paul & Hoenea, a Love Story by Sandy Stewart

My mother was a Southern Belle, or poor white trash, depending on
your point of view. She ruled from a plantation that might be better
described as a shack but carried her beauty with a spark of royalty and
a strong sense of entitlement. She never learned (as would be one day
unearthed by her genealogist granddaughter) that she was a direct
descendent of Charlemagne and his empress, Desiderata, but she
knew in her bones that she deserved to be worshiped and draped in
ermine and jewels! She knew she was "as good as the next person"
and frequently reminded her "girls" of this fact, and that, any

evidence to the contrary; so were they! Perhaps her greatest gift to her descendants was this innate awareness of their singularity. That, and a killer sense of humor and addiction to opulence.

Hoenea sashayed down a Kentucky dirt road one fine day, and with only her barefoot walk and dazzling red hair won the heart of a passing knight who, instantly smitten, vowed to win the heart of yon fine lady. He was a stranger in town, so asked a local about her. Upon learning her name and identity, he declared; "I'm going to marry that girl!" And, so he did. She often told her children that she chose Sir Paul from among her many suitors because "he treated me like a lady," and was the "only boy my daddy trusted to take me out alone in a car." (Daddy Pratt was a drunkard, but he had real good horse sense!)

Paul wasn't the handsomest, richest, or best educated man to court her. (The Pratt girls were popular local beauties who made a game of stealing other girls' beaus.) Paul's armor may have been badly tarnished by dust from the coal mine where he toiled, but he dusted it off, polished it up, and promptly went a'courtin'! He soon won fair lady, then devoted his life to protecting, sheltering, and defending his darling "Mommy Doll" until she died in his arms nearly 60 years later.

Sir Paul and his Lady Hoenea loved each other with such singular devotion that neither could long survive without the other. He cradled her in his arms while she passed gently into the great beyond, then joined her less than a year later. Paul left his own funeral early because Hoenea came to fetch him. (I know; I was there when it happened – right in the middle of the final prayer.) What a hallelujah day of rejoicing that must have been!

Their children, grandchildren, and great grand-children still marvel at the depth and intensity of their love and the strength of their unbreakable connection. At least one of their daughters has frequently wondered if she has ever done anything to deserve that kind of devotion. Happily, she has finally learned that it's not so much about deserving as it is about allowing and returning.

And so it goes................

The Lovely Barefoot Pratt Sisters *(from Sandy Stewart's family photographs)* Thelma with Bible, Hoenea with garden hoe, Lucille with shotgun, and Betty cradling a chicken. They staged the prank photo beside their hen house to send to Lucille's overseas beau, planning to tell him it was her family in front of their Old Kentucky Home. (I'm pretty sure grandma Kate stopped them, because I have the original snapshot!)

Oh, Brother by Sam Watermeier

Before my feet could touch the ground,
before I could read the hands on the clock,
before I could reach great heights . . .
you wanted to name me Superman
before I could be Clark Kent.

You were there.
To see the smoking candles
and hatch marks on the wall.
To pick me up
whenever I would fall.
You were there to poke fun
when I would rhyme.

You were there for the fights,
when the buildings grew bigger,
when I found I could travel on my own.
You were the warm shadow on my back
in the fading after-school sun.

The clock hands flickered,
like the films we watched.
And this whole time, I forgot
you were growing up, too.

Elizabeth by W.B. Cornwell

Lights Out by Kitty O'Doherty

Confession. My electricity was shut off today. Don't worry, it's on now. Still, in all of my bill paying years this has never happened.

It's my fault, I did not pay my bill for, oh apparently, two cycles, and incredibly I didn't even realize it. How this escaped me I do not know. For years I've kept a series of little budget and financial notebooks. I write down what is due, when, and from which paycheck of the month it should come. When I pay, I check it off. It's a system that's worked. Most of my payments are online, but Duke Energy still sends me paper bills, which I normally slice open, peek inside for date and amount due, write that on the front of the envelope, and then record it in my notebook. Normally, anyway. But Duke Energy was forgotten.

For two entire months.

Thinking this morning that I was a day late (which was alarming enough), I called their 800 number not long after getting to work to make my payment immediately. To my surprise, after connecting to my account, I received a recorded message telling me my power had been turned off for lack of payment. Evidently, they'd turned it off shortly after I'd left for work.

I pulled the most recent bill out of my purse and, sure enough, it had been a disconnect notice. I'd missed that notation. I'd think those words would be in bright orange or big letters or something, but they weren't. I'd also missed that the balance due was twice the normal amount. That would've been a clue, had I noticed.

I paid up, following all of the recorded prompts, and got to the point in the recording where they confirm payment and tell me my power will be restored. All was going to be okay until the recording requested that, for safety reasons, I need to go to my breaker box and turn off all switches before the power is turned back on.

Great, I'm at work nearly an hour away, and I now feel without power in two ways. My son and daughter-in-law have house keys but are both at work. Plus, even if I were home, I never go down to the cellar without anyone else in the house. The stairs are steep and it's kind of creepy down there, even when the lights are working.

So naturally I remain calm and focused on a solution.

Hahaha, no, I don't. Nope, not me. I actually start hyperventilating at my desk, suddenly feeling too far away from home, and imagining my 120-year-old house sparking up due to a rare gigantic power surge with my three cats trapped inside.

When I can inhale, I call my coworker into my office. She knows me well and does a pretty great job of putting some rational perspective on the situation. Like, switching everything off is merely a precaution. That the electric company HAS to give this statement because they will not be responsible for any damage. I actually take a full breath by then and wipe my stupid, ridiculous tears, and head toward home to check on things.

Her wisdom gets me almost home until I start obsessing again.

I call my sister on the way and give her the story and then lay out my fears. My food is rapidly spoiling in the fridge, my roof has a smoldering hot spot, my cats are aflame. What if my lack of responsible bill payment has ultimately resulted in a fire that has spread to the homes around me? What if I single-handedly burn down an ENTIRE BLOCK of little historic homes?

My sister breaks my thought pattern and makes me laugh by telling me that in that case, I'd be known as "the Mrs. O'Leary of Noblesville."

I got home and unplugged electronics, although I refused to navigate my way down to the cellar in the dark to fiddle with the breaker box.

As you normal and rational people can already assume, the power came on within a few hours with no fanfare or drama. I reset the clocks, the cats are fine, and nothing's smoking.

I'm going to review my bill paying system and update it, maybe to one of numerous downloadable templates available. And I'll be signing up for auto-pay for all of my utilities. And I will make a therapy appointment very soon, because it seems I really need to work on appropriate responses to unexpected situations.

Women of Noblesville Series of 29 Oil Portraits by Lesley Haflich

"Do one thing every day that scares you"
- Eleanor Roosevelt

This Eleanor Roosevelt quote could sum up a project that I worked on for most of 2018. I'd not really considered myself a portrait painter in the past, yet I was inspired to put paint to canvas for portraits of 29 women in the Noblesville community. From October 3 – October 31, 2018 *The Women of Noblesville* Exhibit was on display in the Stephenson House Gallery at Nickel Plate Arts (at 107 S. 8th Street in Noblesville), where I've been an artist-in-residence for five years. (I'd like to emphasize that the portrait series is just a sampling of dedicated women in town; there are many, many more.)

My inspiration for this project was artist Rose Frantzen, who, upon returning to her hometown of Maquoketa, Iowa, felt disconnected because so many of her friends and family had moved away. Rose set up her easel in a shop on the town square and had the men and women, boys and girls, and even a baby pose for about five hours for each portrait. She completed 180 12x12-inch portraits, which eventually ended up at the Smithsonian. I thought Noblesville was perfect for something similar. When the recent reincarnation of the Women's Movement gained momentum, I thought it would be timely to focus on the women in Noblesville, whose roles have allowed them to contribute significantly to the growing town.

Having only painted two portraits from life previously, I invited a few women I knew to pose at my studio for an hour or so to get them in a favorable light and start a loose painting. I also took some photos, from which I could work later to "get it right." Traditionally, portraits can be somewhat stiff and solemn, and I tried to give mine liveliness with soft, expressive brushstrokes.

The list of women grew from recommendations, and before long I was painting prominent faces in the community, some of whom I'd never met before, and this made me a little nervous, but everyone has been more than nice and accommodating, and it has really been fun talking and getting to know these ladies. The variety and scope of their lives is awesome.

I typed up a short bio about each participant, to hang next to each woman's painting in the exhibit. Included in the show were paintings of educators, medical professionals, attorneys, business owners, government officials, a police detective, a pastor, and – of course – fellow artists. Having lived in Noblesville for 25 years myself, I was impressed by the fact that about half of the women were born and raised here and the rest have chosen to make it their "forever home." Besides getting to connect with the women of Noblesville, this project gave me some new directions and goals in my daily pursuit of art. It also encouraged me to go outside of my comfort zone in more ways than one.

"Forget what the world thinks of you stepping out of your place; think your best thoughts, speak your best words, do your best works, looking only to your own conscience for approval."

- Susan B. Anthony

Me, in my studio. Stephenson House at Nickel Plate Arts. *(Photo by Betsy Reason)*

Dr. Beth Niedermeyer, Superintendent of Noblesville Schools
Dr. Beth Niedermeyer's vast experience has given her determination
to face the challenges of this past year with unrelenting resolve. From
Ft. Wayne, Indiana, Beth comes from a family of teachers and has
devoted her life to education. She received her Bachelor's and
Master's degrees from IPFW, taught most every elementary school
grade aerospace science, and has been a principal before coming to
the Indianapolis area. We are very honored and "super" grateful she
has chosen to lead Noblesville schools into the future. **#millerstrong**

Teresa Peil & Sara Ballew, Owners of Discount Copies
Teresa, who grew up in Princeton, Indiana, moved to Noblesville in
1989 and opened *Discount Copies* in 1996. Twenty-two years later,
this business, which she and her daughter, Sara Ballew, run, is
providing quick, quality printing services to the businesses, clubs, and
people of Hamilton County and beyond. They both are very active in
Tri Kappa, a service organization helping children.

Heidi Karst, Principal at Stony Creek Elementary
Heidi has been the principal at Stony Creek for ten years. Before that, she had been a second and third grade teacher, the NHS girl's athletic director, and a middle and high school assistant principal. She received her Bachelor's degree from Purdue - "Boiler Up" - her Master's from IU, and her administrative licensure program was completed at Indiana Wesleyan University. Her husband is a high school math teacher and her two daughters attend Noblesville schools.

Joanie Weber, Metal Artist
Joanie grew up in Cincinnati, Ohio, where she attended the Academy of Commercial Arts. She began her career as a commercial artist for a typesetting company. Upon moving to Indiana, she took classes at the Indianapolis Art Center in Broad Ripple where she discovered metal sculpting. She worked out of her garage in South Harbour for five years, then set up shop at her studio on S. 8th Street, where she has been creating beautiful sculptures that she sells at art fairs throughout the country.

Lori Schwartz, Schwartz Bait and Tackle/River Custodian
Lori, who was born at Riverview Hospital, cherishes all of her memories connected to the people of Noblesville. She can trace a portion of her roots to the Cherokee, Blackfoot, and Red Blood Indian Tribes. Shortly after high school, she and her husband, Steve bought an old bait shop on Cicero Road, which they have grown throughout the years. She has been active on the Chamber of Commerce (president for 2 years), started the Keep Noblesville Beautiful Campaign, and was instrumental in the cleanup and restocking of White River.

Anita Landress, Preservation Advocate
Anita, who grew up in South Florida, has jumped into the Noblesville preservation scene with both feet. She and her husband are tackling perhaps the biggest restoration project in town, the 3-story white Victorian home on the northeast corner of 9th and Hannibal. She is serving her 4th year as a Noblesville Preservation Alliance board member and enhanced their Fall home tour in 2018 as chairman of the event. It helps that Anita has a love of entertaining and connecting with the community.

Joy Collins, Singer, Realtor, Artist
Joy brings a varied set of talents to Noblesville from Franklin, Indiana, where she was born and raised. She has a degree in graphic design from IU and has spent many years working in the Indianapolis advertising field. Having made the career change to the mortgage industry, Joy is now a real estate broker for F.C. Tucker. You can also hear Joy singing her cool jazz and popular songs around town. Her life motto is, "Fly without wings, learn from mistakes and strive to be good at what you do." Well done, Joy!

Shannon Trump, Deputy Chief of Investigations
Having grown up in Lake County in Northern Indiana, Shannon found
her calling at Indiana University, where she majored in History and
Criminal Justice. She became a police officer in her senior year and
went on to earn her Master's degree in Criminal Justice. Having
worked on the Noblesville police force for 16 years, Shannon has
devoted herself to tirelessly serving the community. By the way, her
grandmother, who drove a semi and a school bus, and her mother,
who put herself through college to become a nurse, are her role
models.

Annie Cook, Realtor

Annie, who was born and raised in Noblesville, went to IU, where she earned her Bachelor's and Master's degrees in education. As a young wife of a law student, she spent three years teaching kindergarten in Bloomington. She and her husband started their family in 1968, first with Matthew, then Craig. She then turned her lifelong passion for real estate into a very successful career selling homes in and around Noblesville for 33 YEARS! Always smiling, Annie is a true "people person."

Debbi Bourgerie, Owner of Rosie's Restaurant
Debbi grew up in St. Louis where she spent many years working in her family's cafeteria. After earning her degree in hotel & restaurant management at Michigan State, and raising a family in Boston and Carmel, Indiana, Debbi opened her first *Rosie's Restaurant* in Noblesville in 2012. She loves the historic atmosphere of the historic Courthouse Square, where *Rosie's* has become the "go to" place for homecooked breakfasts and lunches. The restaurant is named for her grandmother, a role model whose recipes are on the menu.

Mary Sue Rowland, Business Owner, City Council Member, Former Mayor

Mary Sue, who was born and raised in Noblesville, started several businesses here in the early 1970s, including Rowland Printing on N. 9th St. She has been a woman pioneer of community involvement, being the first woman member of the Noblesville Chamber of Commerce, Kiwanis Club, serving three terms on the Noblesville City Council, and was a two-term mayor for the city. Wow!! She has a passion for historic preservation, and her role model was her older sister, Patty Swank (Mrs. Cummings), who taught at the high school for 43 years.

Susan Vincent, Psychotherapist, Owner of Chosen Boutique
Susan, who grew up in Terre Haute, earned her Bachelor's and
Master's Degrees in Marriage and Family Counseling from Indiana
University. She started counseling in Broad Ripple in 1984 and
moved her practice to Noblesville in 1988. With her strong Christian
faith, Susan recently felt called to open her Noblesville boutique
Chosen, where she sells beautiful products made by rehabilitated
female victims of human trafficking, abuse, and poverty.

Rachel Woloshin Wernersbach, Attorney
Rachel grew up in Noblesville, graduated from IU, then received her
law degree from Duquesne Law School in Pittsburgh. After working
for Ray Adler's general practice and a workman's comp firm in
Indianapolis, she returned to Noblesville in 2017 to join Church
Church Hittle and Antrim Law Firm. She looks up to her father, who
runs a successful chiropractic clinic in town, and admires him for his
community involvement. Rachel is on the board for Prevail, Inc., an
agency for women at risk. She is people oriented, and feels she has
strong communication skills, especially through written word.

Leslie Henderzahs, Attorney

From New Albany, Indiana, Leslie received her law degree from IU McKinney. She started as a clerk for Judge Folk and went on to clerk for federal court in Indianapolis. Back in law school, Leslie had become friends with Gayle Schaugenezah. Among few women in their field, they watched out for each other and became very close. Later, Gayle was an attorney at Church Church Hittle and Antrim, and encouraged Leslie to apply. Unfortunately, Gayle passed away from cancer, leaving Leslie to continue her legacy, which led to her becoming the firm's first woman partner.

Kathy Kreag Williams, State Representative, County Clerk
Kathy, who grew up in Noblesville and graduated from Purdue
University, is a former Republican member of the Indiana House of
Representatives, representing the 29th district since 1992. In 2000,
she was elected to the role of Caucus Chair, and in the 2011
legislative session, she played a key role in drawing new redistricting
maps for the Indiana House. In 2018, she became the Hamilton
County Clerk of the Circuit Court. Once named one of five
outstanding women of the state, Kathy has proven her tireless
devotion to serving her constituents.

Judi Johnson, Director of Economic Development (City of Noblesville)

Judi graduated from Purdue in Public Relations and from the Oklahoma University Economic Development Institute. For 10 years, she has led the Noblesville Economic Development Department with the responsibility for management, strategic planning, and business development. She has a proven track record for motivating business and community leaders in their pursuit to bring businesses that generate wealth and job opportunities to Noblesville. She lives with her husband, Roy, and has 29-year-old twins, Kaia and RJ.

Robin Ward, Hamilton County Assessor
Robin Ward was raised in Noblesville and attended IUPUI. She was
first the Noblesville Township Assessor, and 2018 marks her eight
year as the Hamilton County Assessor, assessing commercial and
residential property values. Her husband, Kent Ward, is the county
surveyor. Robin is involved in the MSO Foundation, named for
Megan Ott, who passed away from breast cancer. In her spare time,
Robin likes to exercise and have fun with her large extended family.

Teri Ditslear, Pastor

Teri graduated from Noblesville High School in 1976, and she has learned the ropes from a variety of jobs and real life experiences. She became widowed at one point in her life and met a widower, John Ditslear. Fun fact: their first date was to see Phantom of the Opera (she asked him). As an intern at St. Vincent's Hospice, she watched the chaplains work, her faith strengthened, and she was inspired to go into ministry. Teri eventually attended Anderson University, then Lutheran Seminary in Chicago. She now ministers to her own congregation at her Roots of Life Church on Lakeview Dr. here in town.

Alaina Shonkwiler, Intern Program Director at Noblesville High School

Alaina is from Noblesville; her mom taught at Forest Hill Elementary and her father was and ER nurse and is now Deputy Coroner for Riverview. She graduated from IU in the SPEA Program for Public and Environmental Affairs. She has had a variety of jobs in the community, with the Chamber of Commerce, and the Mayor's Office. She is now in her third year as the program director for Noblesville High School's Internship Program, which places students at various businesses so they get an opportunity to get an idea what their future career path might look like.

Michelle Corrao, Prevail, Inc.

Michelle was working as the marketing director for the Builder's Association in Fort Wayne when, in 1996, her life was changed forever. She was brutally raped by three men as she walked up to her house one night. Detective Arthur Billingsley discovered her and saved her life, but the trauma has required many years of healing. After moving to Noblesville, and seeking therapy at *Prevail, Inc.*, Michelle became more and more involved in their mission to help those who have been victimized. Now the assistant director, she speaks all over the country, and has received a Special Courage Award in Washington D.C.

Dr. Kara Smith, Orthodontist
Kara, who is from West Newton, Indiana, received her Bachelor's
degree in chemistry with a minor in art history. She taught
kindergarten for a year, then headed to Dental School at IUPUI,
Logansport, and then got her Master's in orthodontics. In 2006, she
opened AlignOrthodontics in Noblesville. She enjoys having a small
practice, where she can really get to spend time with her patients.
Kara is also busy with her three young children, ages 9, 7, and 3 (in
2018). She agrees that Noblesville is a great place to raise a family.

Terri Maly, owner, Bellezza Hair Salon
Teri has known that she wanted to be a hair stylist, even as a young
kid growing up in Grand Rapids, Michigan. She started beauty school
in high school and has been doing hair for 44 years. Having grown up
on water, she knew she had to live in South Harbor on Morse Lake
when she moved to Noblesville. Teri opened *Bellezza Hair Salon* 15
years ago. She is always keeping up with new trends and embracing
the new color tints. Teri follows the work of many groundbreaking
stylists, Paul Mitchell being one of her favorites.

Alys Caviness-Gober, Disabled Artist & Writer, Arts Advocate
Alys was born in Ithaca, NY while her father earned his PhD at
Cornell University. Their family moved to Noblesville in the 1970s.
Alys taught Anthropology, Women's Studies, and ESOL at Ball State
University. Her arts business is *Creative Expressions Arts*, and she is
an ordained minister for her non-denominational 501(c)(3) spiritual
organization, *Sacred Heart of the Rose*. Alys is a Juried Artist in the
Hamilton County Artists' Association, and founded *Logan Street
Sanctuary, Inc.* Her many passions include family, raising awareness
for hidden disabilities, and supporting the arts and other artists.

Julia Kozicki, Attorney, Mayoral Candidate
Having grown up in Noblesville, attending Forest Hill Elementary
and Noblesville H.S., Julia has always been dedicated to this
community. She has served for several years on the Noblesville
School Board and volunteered for Tri Kappa and the United
Methodist Church. Julia is the national legal counsel for Sigma Kappa
Sorority and has also held leadership positions with the Indiana State
Bar Association and the Hamilton County Leadership Academy. Just
this past August (2018), Julia announced that she is going to run for
Mayor of Noblesville. Her qualifications speak for themselves. Good
Luck, Julia!

Martha Gascho, Attorney

Martha was born and raised in Noblesville and still lives in the house that she grew up in. She graduated from Butler with a degree in English and taught English at Tech High School for some years. She decided to study law at IU in Indianapolis and received her degree in 1973. Webb & Webb Law Firm on the north side of the Noblesville Square gave Martha her start (along with many other local attorneys). In 1980, she opened her own firm on the south side of the square. She has been involved in many areas of law, and today she focuses mainly on wills and estate planning and distribution. What a great legacy for our town!

Kay Richards, Artist

Kay went to high school in Crown Point, Indiana, where she was the editor of the school newspaper. That led to a scholarship to IU, then a Master's degree from Butler. She taught journalism and was a counselor at Lawrence Central High School. While raising her two daughters here in Noblesville, she wrote publicity for every volunteer organization in town. One passion has always been art, and she is an accomplished watercolorist. After completing her current two-year term as president of the Hamilton County Artists' Association at the end of 2018, Kay looks forward to future personal and professional development.

Janina Pettiford, LPN, Events Planner
Janina was a "military brat," born in Germany. Later, her family
settled in Indiana at Grissom Air Reserve Base. She has worked as an
EMT Basic in 911, private transport and emergency transport.
Currently, she is an LPN working in blood plasma, and she is also the
offsite events planner for *Love's Hangover Creations* in Noblesville.
Her passion is to make the world a better place for future generations.

Betsy Reason, Editor Noblesville Times
Betsy graduated from Shenandoah High School and received her Bachelor's degree in journalism and sociology from Franklin College. After reporting in various departments for the *Noblesville Daily Ledger*, Betsy went on to be a reporter for the *Indianapolis Star*. In June of 2014, she returned to Noblesville to take the job of editor of the *Noblesville Times*, and we're so glad she is back home doing what she loves.

Kelli Ray Yates, Singer, Guitarist, Barista Extraordinaire
Kelli graduated from Carmel H.S. and studied English at IUPUI.
Eleven years ago, she discovered what a charming town Noblesville
was and decided to move here. Soon after, she got a job at Noble
Coffee & Tea, where she has been serving espressos and other
delicious coffee drinks ever since. Meanwhile, she learned guitar and
became part of the group *Noble Roots*, which performed at many
venues including art fairs. Recently, Kelli began a new chapter of her
life by having a little baby girl, Rory (Congratulations, Kelli!), and
performing as one-half of the female duo, *Mama's Homemade*.

Moon Song by Alys Caviness-Gober

22:22 by Maren Thornbury

Eventually
she wasn't scared of cracking doors
and closed voices.
The girl giggled; the girl broke,
oh how
I should have known.

Eventually
men won't hide their fear of eyes so
far less than their fear of
god, and questions:
what if we are not in control?
Should I have known?

Eventually
I wouldn't taste blood after the hours trickle down
my back and the shower ticks by.
She was breath and I said
"Okay" said,
"that's okay,"

and eventually
I will learn to swim in the hurt, but deep within me now
at the bottom of a dumb old high school
swimming pool
I will cry oh, cry
how I should have known.

Accept the Mystery by Sam Watermeier

I saw *A Serious Man* a decade ago, and I'll never forget how I felt during its final moments.

The closing sequence captures the enormous dread that sometimes looms over everyday life. It shows how receiving an ominous phone call from a doctor can feel like the universe caving in on you.

I knew that feeling all too well when this film was released in the fall of 2009. I was fresh out of high school and completely unsure of my future. My dad was home after nearly a year in the hospital, but our house was full of its remnants – feeding tubes, Fentanyl patches, etc. Like Larry Gopnik, the hero of *A Serious Man*, we struggled to cope with a surreal new normal.

One of the Coen Brothers' best films, *A Serious Man* follows this meek physics professor as he's beset by marital, professional, and ethical dilemmas amid the morally murky atmosphere of the late 1960s. The film's Midwestern setting exudes an eerie calm that mirrored the mood of our neighborhood that fall.

As my brother and I sat in the Keystone Art Cinema watching this masterpiece unfold, its mounting tension overwhelmed us. It was as if the stress of the past year had been compressed into 106 minutes.

In the final sequence, Larry adds a medical concern to his ever-growing number of problems as a tornado swirls outside his son's school. The film abruptly ends during this masterful sequence of suspense. The sharp cut to black left me in a panic. But it was an *invigorating* panic – an urge to escape and start embracing life as quickly as possible.

Although *A Serious Man* ends on a bleak note, it's also oddly life-affirming. By showing that what we have can be swept away in an instant, it made me want to hold on to good times more tightly and not take anything for granted. It also compelled me to stop letting worries prevent me from living in the moment. At the time, I couldn't help but wonder what the future would hold for me and my family. But, as one of the film's characters says, I had to "accept the mystery."

Many Coen Brothers films share that sentiment. *The Big Lebowski* is largely about going where the wind takes you and warding off negativity along the way. "You can't be worried about that shit, man. Life goes on," the laidback Jeff "the Dude" Lebowski says.

In one of the segments from the Coens' latest film, *The Ballad of Buster Scruggs*, a character utters, "Uncertainty. That is appropriate for matters of this world." He goes on to experience a devastating loss, but at least his embrace of uncertainty allowed him to appreciate the calm before the storm.

As my mom often says, "Take things one day at a time." I felt like she was speaking through the Coen Brothers with *A Serious Man*'s opening title card, which reads, "Receive with simplicity everything that happens to you." I carry that lesson with me to this day.

Lying On The Moon (Plus One) by Alys Caviness-Gober

Constellations by Mama's Homemade

(song lyric; written by Kelli Ray Yates and Kat Wedmore)

On a bed of grass
Starin' at the black
A million points of light, all within my sight
Bring me back to me

Constellations, memories
Connecting stars and I can see
I am her, she is me

Light comes and goes
I live with ghosts
The moments in the sky, reflected in my mind
Take me back to who I've been

Found the perfect tree
Sat just out of reach
Street lights tell the time, the night was yours and mine
And we ran

Constellations, memories
Connecting stars and I can see
I am her, she is me
Flooding back their light to me
Creating shadows and I can see
I am her, she is me

Found a need for you
Love out of the blue
Your mixtape in my car, now that is all we are
Why did I run

Stars run all around the sky
Sometimes their paths collide (I keep coming back to this, all the
chances that I missed)
Sometimes the stars align

Constellations, memories
Connecting stars and I can see
I am her, she is me
Flooding back their light to me
Creating shadows and I can see
I am her, she is me

Do Not Get On That Horse by Brenda VandeWater

"Whatever you do, do NOT get on that horse!"

I was ten years old and I was on the outside of the fence. Ol' Monon, our young thoroughbred race horse was on the other.

He was gorgeous. I was obsessed with him from the moment I watched him born. His mother, Helen Z, was a beautiful gray mare and Ol' Monon looked just like her.

I would trail after my dad every morning to feed the horses just to get a chance to pet his nose. I watched every day as my dad and our trainer, Scout, worked with him. Taught him to walk with the halter and bit, then added the blanket, and then the saddle.

There was more walking him with the saddle. All along the fence row – for what seemed like forever to me. I would join them. Walk with them. Pat Ol' Monon's rump when I was told I could. Sometimes, Scout would let me help groom him at the end of the day.

I loved him. And I was sure he loved me.

"Whatever you do, do NOT get on that horse!"

Let's be clear. I had ridden a LOT of horses. At any given time, we had at least four or five horses. Plus, we had two ponies. I had ridden the ponies, Feller and Trigger, unsupervised many times. After passing the "saddling test," I was cleared to ride them whenever I wanted.

I had ridden the retired horses several times. Helen Z would let me ride her all over the back pastures. Of course, these rides were with western saddles. You know, the saddles with the horn at the front, long stirrups, and a full saddle.

But my dad and Scout were training Ol' Monon to be a race horse.

Is that really all that different? My 10-year old mind did not really see a difference. I mean his mom let me ride her – all the time.

So that day, my dad and Scout had saddled Ol' Monon. They were talking, but I wasn't paying attention. I was busy patting Ol' Monon's nose. He liked it.

My dad and Scout stopped talking. My dad looked at me and said, "Do NOT get on that horse!"

Apparently, all I heard was, "GET ON THAT HORSE!"

Dad and Scout went into the barn. I looked around. Nobody but me and Ol' Monon out here. I rubbed his nose and he neighed. Seemed like he was saying, "Come on. Let's go for a ride."

I climbed up over the fence and dropped to the other side. Ol' Monon snuffled a little. I was pretty sure he was happy to see me.

I waited a second – maybe two. Then decided, Ol' Monon and I should go for a ride. Imagine how happy my dad and Scout would be to see a rider up on him.

I had maneuvered Ol' Monon closer to the fence, so I could use it to get my foot in the stirrup. He seemed fine with it. Another sign that he was happy to have me up.

I climbed on the fence, put my foot in the stirrup, and swung myself up on Ol' Monon.

For a brief moment, all was fine. Then suddenly, it wasn't. Ol' Monon reared up, pulling his lead free from the fence. I then realized, all too late, that I had never seen anyone seated on Ol' Monon.

He took off bucking and whinnying, all over the barnyard. I was holding on for dear life. I could hear Dad yelling for me to hang on. I could see Scout, out of the corner of my eye, trying to grab the lead while avoiding Ol' Monon's hooves.

The barnyard was spinning, as Ol' Monon ran and bucked. Then suddenly, I was airborne. I was flying through the fencing around the chicken coup.

After I landed, I opened my eyes to see Ol' Monon continue his bucking bronco routine to the back pasture with Scout chasing after.

I looked up to find both my dad and mom crouched over me.

"Are you okay?" my dad asked.

I took a quick assessment. My right wrist hurt and when I looked down at it . . . it was bent a little bit to the right – and not in a good way. That's when I felt it. The tears began to flow and my mom held me close to comfort me.

"It's not bad," she said. "We will get that taken care of and you'll be good as new before you know it."

I looked up and my dad was scowling down at me.

"What did I say?"

Snuffling through tears, I said, "What?"

Very sternly, he said, "What did I say?"

Mom said, "Can't this wait?"

His glare was the only reply she needed.

He repeated, "What did I say?"

Summoning up my courage as well as my best "poor pitiful me" voice, "Do not get on that horse."

"And what did you do?"

"I got on the horse."

He looked at me, then at Mom. "Is it serious?"

She examined my wrist. "Her wrist is probably broken. But that's all that seems to be wrong."

He nodded and said, "Okay, then. Wait here."

Mom helped me up and navigated us over the chicken coup fencing. We were headed toward the house when Dad walked around the corner of the barn with Helen Z saddled.

He said, "Okay. Come on over. You get thrown, you get back on."

Mom protested, "But she probably has a broken wrist. Can't that wait?"

He dipped his head and said in a low voice,

"I told her. Do NOT get on that horse. She got on the horse. She got thrown. Now, she gets back on. She has to learn to get back up. She has to learn that you don't stay down. She has to learn that there may not always be someone to pick you back up. She has to get back up."

Mom led me back to Helen Z. Dad boosted me up. He led me around the paddock. Clutching my wrist, I cried the whole time. It was a slow, plodding walk. But with every hoof beat, I felt the throb in my wrist. And when we got back to the pasture gate, Dad lifted me down.

An ER visit and a new cast later, Dad was sitting on the porch swing.

He called me out, and patted the swing.

He took a sip of his coffee and asked, "What did you learn?"

I said, "When you say don't get on the horse, don't get on the horse."

He smiled and said, "Yes. What else?'

It took me a minute. Then, I got it.

"Get back up!"

Green With Envy by Leslie Ober

I fell in love at a drive-thru by Maren Thornbury

I fell in love at a drive-thru
Stopping for cheap coffee on my way to a job I didn't love or want.
I was thinking about my bed back home, how it was waiting for me,
counting the hours on my
chapped fingers and breaking it down.
Like
Eight hours; which means two blocks of four hours; which means I
just have to get through one
hour four times, and thirty minutes eight times, and ten minutes three
times eight times four
times two times, only eight hours left in this shitty day.
I'm not really a coffee drinker you see.
I liked sugar and chocolate and sweet.
But I was so damn tired, and I stayed up too late counting hours
again,
and maybe it could get me through the day.
So I pulled off the highway, and the GPS I used
(despite knowing the way)
screamed at me as they do.
You know the voice,
"Proceed to the route, proceed to the route, proceed to the . . ."
Sometimes when I feel sorry for myself I play the game
At Least I'm Not . . .
Helps me ground myself, makes me stop taking life for granted.
Like that I've got money for a GPS to tell me when to make a left.
So as I sat in my heated car, waiting for my turn,
"At least I'm not a fast food worker."
"At least I get paid more than $6 an hour."
"At least I went to college"
"At least I can eat"
"At least my parents love me"
"At least at least at least"

"Hi welcome to _____ how can I help you today?"

My head snapped back to reality, oh right, I was drinking coffee
today.
But that voice . . . oh, what a voice!

Cracking and shaking through a box, covered in bird shit and gum.
Bright and fake and detached from body.
My heart felt like it might explode out of my chest, with a voice like that.
"Hello?"
Oh, yes, hello.
I ordered a coffee and dug out the change and pulled up to the second window please and
thank you
(almost dropped the quarters but saved it in a badass way you shoulda seen it)
and I proceeded to the route and I went to work and the whole way there and the whole way
home I was . . .
I was SMILING.
So hard it hurt my cheeks and my boss asked me if I was alright and damn girl it was a voice
from a box!
But it truly was a wonderful voice.
And even though they forgot the sugar,
Even though they gave me a small instead of a large,
Even though the bitter taste almost made me pull over and throw up my breakfast.
I went back the next day
And the day after that
After that too
Listening to that cracking shaking voice; smiling, making a little more conversation each time
Stupid stuff about the weather and the traffic and the terrible taste of coffee.
Holding up the line, trying my hardest to get a chuckle out of the cracking and shaking,
sometimes a full laugh.
I fell in love at a drive-thru, honey,
And maybe it was just a voice, maybe that's what made it so easy, the safety of it all.
I could not see the sweat stains,
the grease dripping off a forehead,
the heat of a grill in the back of a dirty kitchen,
crooked teeth or squinty eyes or a round belly.

Maybe there was a kind of freedom in flirting with a box.
In finding a routine that made me happy for the rest of the day.
In buying cheap coffee and dumping it out the window.
In the caffeine that stems from good conversation.
Maybe it was also lonely.
And one day,
after a casual mention of an emptiness so deep you could drown in it,
the cup was the right size,
and came with sugar,
it didn't taste like crap,
and there was a number written on the sleeve.
But
I fell in love with an idea.
And here before me, the idea threatened me to become real.

So,

I dropped the quarters and did not catch them in time.
I did not smile the whole way to work and the whole way home.
My stomach hurt so bad that my boss asked me if I was alright today,
and I was too sick to
shake my head.
It was no longer just a voice from a box, a wonderful crackling voice,
and as my fingers hovered over the buttons I could not find my own.
I forced my hand to stop shaking, forced myself to take deep breaths,
but this was not a drive-thru anymore.
There was no shaking and cracking, or imagined smiles behind a glass
gate,
or fluttering of butterflies as I could put a face to a voice.
It was real. And I was afraid.
So I put down the phone.
And even though they remembered the sugar.
Even though they gave me the right size
Even though it tasted like heaven in a sip
Even though there was a happiness there, for the first time in many
years.
Even though I had fallen in love.
I listened to the GPS and didn't stop for cheap coffee.
I imagined a voice.
Sitting, smiling, waiting and waiting and waiting . . .

I imagined grease and sweat and heat and $6 an hour.
I imagined lives far shittier than mine, imagined the possibility I
could make things better,
imagined mattering to someone.
And I shuddered.
And I pressed on the gas.
And I blew a stop sign.
I pulled into a Starbucks
I paid $6 for a cup of coffee and a clear voice from a fancy screen.
I took a sip, and it . . .
It tasted like good coffee.
And maybe my taste buds were too used to the taste of shit,
maybe I grew to like the lack of sugar and the wrong size,
maybe it was the hint of a smile in the drink,
a pinch of happiness,
an escape from loneliness.

But it was disgusting.

Unbecoming by Rachel Cox

I fall
Fall so low I become part of the ground
Or it becomes part of me
Such great heights I thought I reached
Such great heights I thought I reached
Then a breeze came along

But this day of decay
Will sprout seeds for harvest
I rake myself
a bed of acid leaves
Take me,
I tell them, break me
down and make me more

For what could I ever learn up on that branch?

Kee by Bryony Stanger

Smoke by Maik Strosahl

It is a good smoke
Rising from this fire,
Filled with the stories
Of our fathers
And our father's fathers,
Those who
Chased the buffalo,

Those who fought
The men taking what was
Not theirs and
Not ours
For themselves.

It was a great smoke
My father shared with me,
His father by his side,
Burning the white man's tobacco,
Letting its billow rise
To mingle with their words,
Bringing color
To images I
Could barely fathom.

It is a good smoke,
From hard wood
Meant to reach
The hard heads of sons
And the sons of sons who
Are no longer listening,
Want nothing to do
With the old ways
And the stories of old men –
Of this old man –
Rising into the sky,
A good smoke unheard
As it is lost to the clouds.

A Visit to Grandma's House by Dorothy "Dottie" Zeiss Young

One gray winter afternoon, when my mood was a gray as the weather, I took an alternate route home from Indianapolis after a day of teaching Middle School kids Art. My meandering took to me past my Grandmother's former home, on River Road, a home she reluctantly left in 1963, after suffering a stroke. My Grandpa Bill, her second husband, had died in 1961, from pancreatic cancer, discovered during an appendectomy. We tried to let he stay in her home; we hired people to stay with her; many in worse shape than she was. We felt comforted that least she had company, "out in the sticks." After the last companion died and she suffered another mild stroke she came to stay with us, Mom, Dad, and me. I was in high school at the time and of course I "knew everything." I was a bit embarrassed by my Grandmother and her old-fashioned ways. I didn't appreciate her when I was younger, but I do now. How lonely she must have been.

Despite my lack of appreciation for Grandma's old-fashioned ways, I loved her so – and I love her still; she was tiny and tough; a silver-haired dynamo, her braided hair wrapped her head like clasped hands. She taught me to braid by tacking three strips of material on her dining room door, she demonstrated and left me to finish the job. I know how to braid very well. She would let me brush and braid her long hair for hours.

When I would stay with her in the summer we would wash our hair then go outside in the cow pasture and brush our tresses until they were dry. I still reflect on that time; the sun warm on our faces – the wind blowing the tall grasses and our hair. When we were done, we would go back in the house and braid each other's hair.

I was coming near Grandma's house, I pulled into the driveway under the Buckeye tree, the house was still standing – not proudly, but in some sort of defiance to the elements. The gravel pit across the road bought the property after her death, she never wanted them to get it because she knew what would happen, but her oldest son sold it. The gravel company was across the road from the house. I remember sleeping on the sofa with the door open and would wake up to the *shook-ka, shook-ka* sound of the machinery; sorting the gravel and the rumble of dump trucks passing by, they make more noise when they are empty. We were always grateful when the work day was over and the quiet came back.

I hesitated to go in the house that was now the office for the gravel company, but I did. I told them how my Grandmother Jessie used to live in the house. Their office was in the front room of the house, the room she used for a bedroom. Their desk was where her feather bed used to rest. I asked permission to look around; everything was the same. They had paneled some of the rooms and the floor sagged at an incredible angle, but I could close my eyes and see where all the furniture had been. The living room wall opposite the windows was where her lawyers bookshelves, holding rows of books protected by glass doors stood, *Song of Bernadette*, Art History, biographies *ad infinitum*, keys to the Kingdom of knowledge. Grandmother used to give book reviews to clubs and write articles and devotions for *The Daily Ledger*, our local paper. At one of her book reviews at Forest Park, she asked me to give a book review and I told them about *Goldilocks and the Three Bears*. I was a hit!

Grandma didn't drive, she had to depend on friends or a taxi, so these books were her link to the distant far away places she dreamed of. She once visited her brother Ernest, in Santa Barbara, California. Ernest was a publisher of a periodical called *Club Magazine*. He encouraged her love of writing by arranging for her to present a scenario for a movie and got it published. It was a parallel of her own life. The heroine was a woman named Jetta, a nickname of Jessie's. Jetta's young husband had died at age 39, as had Jessie's own husband, of typhoid, leaving her and four boys to raise. Jetta had a selfish father-in-law, as did Jessie, He was very stern and very frugal, keeping control over all monies spent. Her scenario never sold.

Jessie would never forget that her husband Parker had promised to send her to Madam Blaker's teachers college in Indianapolis the next year, but he died. So books were her outlet. She had played the female lead, Portia, in her senior play, *The Merchant of Venice*, at the Wild's Opera House in Noblesville. She loved learning, creating, and performing, she wrote poems – honest ones of her love of nature, her boys, and her struggles to comprehend the reasons she felt God challenged her so sorely.

I passed into the dining room, scene of so many memorable Sunday meals. The table always bulged from the bounty of the farm; chicken and noodles, homemade bread, corn, green beans, and peach pie with a sugar glaze. I could reach into my memory and almost smell the aromas; I could see Grandma in her apron, the flowery printed pinafore kind that had pockets and a ruffle around the neck, waiting for raves from the appreciative diners. Dad with his usual comment of

"Mother, I don't think this is up to your standards," which we all recognized as a lighthearted lie, a sort of back handed compliment.

As I walked into the kitchen, I felt like I must be in some kind of time warp. The wallpaper was the same, a formerly a white background with a 1950s vintage kitchen still life with little kettles and fruit. I hesitated at the broom closet for a moment, opening the door slowly, half hoping that Grandpa Bill's army green work coat and hat would still be there, and that his shotgun would be propped in the corner of the closet, ready for action if needed for skunks or other varmints. There were only rags and mops. That's all.

The bathroom was unkempt, but the same as it had been when the fixtures were put in. The bathtub was square and huge, it was an odd green color. We didn't have an indoor bathroom until I was nine, so this wonder seemed like a swimming pool to me. Each night when I stayed at Grandma's, she would tuck me in, and she would ask, "do you have to piddledeewink"? It was a joke between us. Even with this newfangled convenience in their home, Bill and Jessie kept a commode or slop jar under a commode chair in their bedroom.

With trepidation I managed the courage to go upstairs, that forbidden territory of old. The upstairs was unheated and had a closed staircase. The only time it was used was in the summer when my cousin Ronnie Parker would come and help farm. We all called him Parker. I climbed the steep incline, remembering how terrified I was as a child; what hid in the recesses of this unknown space? I looked in all the closets and corners. The ancient wallpaper, hung no doubt when the house was built in the 1800s, whispered echoes of another time, one that seemed to me to be calmer and gentler.

Parker's room was at the top of the stairs facing east, directly over Grandmother's room. There were books and magazines scattered about; I picked some up. One particularly old book was entitled, *The Music Lover*. I opened it and found an inscription written to my Grandfather, "to Bill from Jessie, Christmas 1903," a long-forgotten gift, a message of regard now retrieved and cherished again. The gravel office allowed me to take the book. The house is now gone, but I can still recognize the trees on the property, and I'm grateful for the much-needed gift I received on that gray dreary day.

If I Knew Then by Gail Mehlan

Tell Me A Story by Brenda VandeWater

As far back as I can remember
Our family history you would tell
But my recollection seems to be spotty
The details – I don't know too well

I have wisps, and pieces, and tidbits
But the tales that I should have known
Escape me – I was just looking forward
Never realizing your words were on loan

Suppose I close my eyes and pretend
That I could ask of your life before me
I know you'd turn with your eyes all a-twinkle
Then smile and reply . . . "Well, let's see…"

I would say – paint me so vivid a picture
That I believe I can see you at play
Let me experience your childhood adventure
Make me a part of the mischief that day

Then tell me my favorite story
How the two of you met and just knew
That happy ever after could happen
That life's always better with two

I wish I knew more of your young life
The newlyweds, your struggles, your trials
The little things that made you both stronger
All the moments that made it worthwhile

Please weave me the cloth of this family
Use every color and stitch every thread
Making the fabric so clear and so brilliant
That we can see every story when spread

I would bring out this quilt for my children
Shake it out, watch the memories drift
To explain to them just where they come from
To remind them that family's a gift

So, if this lesson you still have not learned
Then, here is a word to the wise
On earth, no instrument exists
To measure how fast the time flies

On Wisdom by D.L. Dasher

Age grants us grains of wisdom
Though scarce and thin and widely scattered,
The precious kernels that we find can matter
If we sincerely, humbly glean them.

Some of us never reap these grains
In pride and ignorance they are content,
Foregoing wisdom's nourishment
They stagnate and remain unchanged.

But with wisdom, there is a cost
Its lens lets us see clearly
That much of what we harmed or lost
Were things we loved most dearly.
And, oh, the pain that comes along
With knowing how often we were wrong.

In time our chargers begin to fade
We linger briefly in some scarce shade
We wish to stay, but long ago our choice was made
We struggle but go on.

We creep along, with little left
Years of wandering in wilderness
Gave much excitement, but little joy or rest
Barely we slog on.

At last we are completely spent.
And now we ponder how we spent
Our fleeting lives, and what they meant.
We can no longer travel on.

No marker marks our stopping place
No poet sings of our breathless chase
We rest, now in God's sweet grace
To greener fields we now go on.

Red's Tractor by Al Geisler

A memoir in photographs . . .

Red's Tractor was a working tractor, a 1948 International Harvester FarmAll Super A. Grandpa "Red" Geisler grew fruit and vegetables on the family farm. Red's Tractor was used to prepare and plant lawns. I have many memories of working the tractor with my grandfather and father.

Red's Tractor was all about work. Pull, Plow, Disc, Dig, Till, Float, Plant, and Harvest.

In 2018 Red's red tractor was restored for a life of retirement and play. Parades and Joy Rides. Red's Tractor proudly ran in the 40th Noblesville Christmas parade.

Red's Tractor, 1950. Nelson and Lois Geisler on the family farm in Benton Harbor, MI. (*Original photograph by Ruth Geisler, from Geisler family photos*).

Red's Restored Tractor, 2018. Al Geisler on the restored tractor, in Noblesville, IN. (*photograph by Gail Geisler, from Geisler family photos*)

The Fix by Ellen Santasiero

Bum years, the early eighties were, for cars anyway, Gil thought, and the one he was trying to fix the day Veena came to work at Fikey Tire was no exception. Lincoln Town car, 1981. Mrs. Grant brought it in every few months for something or other. Its electronic system was addled, and every time they waved good-bye to Mrs. Grant, Mike said, "Thing'll be back before we know it, springing its nuts."

Gil was pitched forward under the hood of the Lincoln when Mike brought his cousin Veena to meet him and Gene. It was the ignition with the Lincoln, but when Gil saw Mike and a pretty woman approach him, he suddenly thrust his hands between the sooty cables and canisters and pretended to be changing the plugs. He didn't want to have to shake hands because his hands trembled and he only had four fingers on his right hand. He'd forgotten to grab a wrench, so he just gripped two plugs and pretended to unscrew.

"This here's Veena," Mike said. "New office girl."

Business had gotten so's that no one had a free hand to answer the phone anymore. Gil nodded at Veena, said hello, then looked down at the place where his hands disappeared into the car's works. "Nice to meet you," he said, looking up quickly, keeping the exclamation point of his body doubled over, until they passed off to Gene. Mike winked. He knew the Lincoln didn't need plugs.

In the weeks before the morning Veena arrived, Gil had been having strange dreams. One that stayed on his mind for most of a morning was where he'd been out in his yard at night and there was the Roundtable from the King Arthur legend – he couldn't see it but he knew it was near. Milky white knights stood all over his lawn, and one of them, Arthur, he guessed, came up to him, pointed, and said, "You." He felt himself begin to move towards Arthur, but then the dream folded itself up like a game board and twisted out of sight. In the mornings, he'd looked out over his yard, trying to match what he saw in the dream with his real yard. He imagined the knights there briefly, a few had been clustered near the place his ex-wife Joanne had stood a year ago and let her wedding ring rip through the air and flip against Gil's chest. He'd sit for a while thinking about her, but then realize he was late. He'd busy himself with getting out the door and wonder why he'd lost track of time thinking about her, seeing that that was a year ago, and he had long since gotten over that.

Gil liked being a mechanic. It was hard work, steady, with lots of different things to do every day. One of his great pleasures was to clap a car's hood down after fixing it, and drive it out onto the lot. He wore a blue all-in-one suit and brown Red Wings. He was bigger and taller than Mike, and tended to gain weight if he didn't watch. Big-chested and narrow-hipped, he had a football player's body, but not a football player's heart, which his gum-chewing high school coach soon found out. But since he had mass and his unsmiling face intimidated opposing players, the coach asked him to keep playing anyway, and Gil had agreed.

He'd worked for fifteen years at Fikey Tire. He'd sometimes arrive first and unlock the doors, switch on the lights, and start the coffee. Next he'd flip on the radio and wait for a few minutes, sitting in the green vinyl swivel chair at Mike's desk in the front of the place. He'd sit and think while the smells of oil and rubber became less distinct the more he breathed them, and the level of the coffee rose to fill the glass pot. That would all change now that Veena was there. It would be her job to open the shop.

One morning, about a week before Veena came, as he sat there in the office waiting, he had this feeling that everything was in its right place. Nothing seemed strained, or on its way to something else. No animals were rooting, for God's sake. The leaves on the trees were as broad and green as they'd ever be, and the sun was as high and warm as it had aspired to all spring and early summer. Gil felt peace, riveted to the details of the morning, to his body and the chair in which he sat, the way he felt when his mind was drawn down into his hands and his thighs after the second shot of whiskey.

But now Veena was here.

Evenings after work, Gil usually had supper at the same bar. Oftentimes his friend Rollo met him there. Rollo worked at the Ace and sometimes gave Gil advice about how to get a woman. One night Rollo brought Gil a copy of the book *Creative Ways to Ask For a Date*. "Have someone help you put the person's car on blocks," read Rollo, "not too high, because you want the person to get into the car and not be able to leave before they notice. When they get out of the car and look under, they see your note: *Hi! Now that I have your attention, how would you like to attend the ____ with me?*"

Rollo was married to June, a small woman with dark hair. Rollo often said things that were no more helpful than his jokes, things like *show them the palace, Gil, show them your kingly offerings.* Tonight, while he and Rollo drank beer and waited for their food, Gil told Rollo about Veena.

"Got some new help down at the shop."

Gil reached for a napkin and covered the empty space on the table in front of him.

"S'at right?" Rollo said, watching the waitress put plates on the table. Gil watched Rollo's eyelids snap open and shut in anticipation, watched him shake dressing on his salad and pile ketchup next to his fries, and he decided he would say no more about the new office person. He was tired. He felt his interest in Veena rising up inside him – had felt it all week – but he was not quite up to it. He was not quite ready ride something like this, follow it out to wherever it might lead.

At the end of that week, Veena's first week at Fikey Tire, came a tornado warning. Gil wasn't worried, they had warnings all the time in the summer in southern Indiana, but he cracked his windows anyway before he went to the bar, in case it got serious and the little house needed to let a bit of the storm in to keep itself from getting blown over. He looked outside and saw an awning that had been battered in the last storm still waiting to be fixed. His jaw tensed.

Outside, the sky was pea green. The television in the bar droned on in staticky knots. Gil remembered his morning alone in Mike's office. Whatever that moment was in Mike's office, he wanted it back. He wanted Rollo to stop devouring the food with his eyes. He wanted the sky to not be piss-full and ready to burst. He didn't want to have to move towards something, towards the white knight in the dream, towards Veena. Things move towards you anyway, Gil thought, and if you could just be still, maybe they'd go by without touching you, or not hurt so much when they did.

Flight by Maik Strosahl

Those days of flight
Still come to me in slumber,
Two souls unbound by gravity,
Two wings joined by hands
Through the mists and
Breaking free into clear blue
Eyes shining with wonder

As to what we would see,
Where would we go together?

If we had known
Our time was to be short,
That turboprops spin and
Slice the seconds away,
Would we still have chanced
To dream the sky?

Our flight still comes to me,
Played on movie screen eyelids,
And I can still feel
The flutter of weightlessness,
The touch of
Flying through the heavens as one
Without regret.

Lava by Alys Caviness-Gober

To The Mother Rabbit Who Lives Under Our Deck by Bonita Cox Searle

I see you
through our kitchen window,
quivering under the bird
feeder,
waiting for sustenance to drift
down
as the mourning doves enjoy
their feast of seeds and grain.

I wash other people's casserole
dishes,
their names Sharpied on the
bottoms
and imagine your children
oblivious
in the shallow nest
that you pawed for them under
our deck.

I want to know,
do you have hopes
for your children,
their blind eyes with no sense
of direction
and their defenseless pink skin
with
no fur to protect them
from the fickle winds?

Do you wake
terrified
that your milk won't nourish
them,
that your body warmth won't
reach

their center,
that your nudges and nuzzles
and shared wisdom
are not enough?

Do you worry that
one little kit will be her own
danger,
her protective fur unable to
grow,
and her hazel eyes
refusing to see the light?

If that happens,
I promise,
the mourning doves
will drift down beside you,
bringing
sustenance
in glass casseroles.

One Good Man by Jean Roberts
(*song lyric*)

One good man, one good man
Doin the best he can
All I really needed was just one good man

When I was young and I was strong
I wanted to make it on my own
I did okay but I was all alone
What I really needed was one good man

One good man, one good man
Doin the best he can
What I really needed was one good man

Now in our life we lasted long
By doin right not doin wrong
We do our best, the best we can
Cause what I needed was one good man

One good man, one good man
Doin the best he can
All I really needed was my one good man

Look around what's going on
In our confusion we don't know where to go
We'll lose it all 'til nothing left to show
What we really need is just one good man

One good man, one good man
Doin the best he can
What we really need is just one good man

One good man, one good man
Doin the best he can
What we really need is just one good man

Luna's Summer by Paul "Spike" Morin-Wilson

Her eyes confused little clouds
      beneath wrinkled brow's tension;
they rained doubt
      on pages that meant nothing,
stormed above a mouth that said,
      "Uncle, I'll never learn to read."

Now so clear,
      shining pride at Mom and Dad,
precious twin stars
      above the curve of a voice,
reading aloud now,
      loudest of all.

Shine on, little girl.

Rusty Heart by Alys Caviness-Gober

Tearstained Pillows by W.B. Cornwell

Days full of watching happy couples,
longing for someone to call my own.

That one person that would hold my hand,
and smile at the thought of me.

Watching, enviously, I must admit, at the lovers in movies,
wondering if these lips of mine would ever know a kiss.

Walls were built. My self-esteem withered.
Tears stained my pillow.

I hoped and prayed to be loved by someone,
that someday I would be what someone was looking for.

Years came and went and I remained alone,
I realized that a life of solitude would be my destiny.

Had I known that one sunny April day, it would all change,
that one day I would have her in my life.

Maybe I wouldn't have been prepared for such a blessing,
perhaps I wouldn't know what a precious jewel I now possess.

Had I not waited so long, and given up,
my "when you least expect it" moment would never have come.

But she did come! She came and showed me, love,
and she tore down the walls brick by brick.

She made me see that I had self-worth,
making me feel special and treasured in ways I never thought
possible.

My pillows no longer know tears,
but most importantly I know her love.

Morning Musings by Maren Thornbury

She used to pretend to smoke cigarettes
behind the dumpsters out back of the theater,
alternating between drags and
bites of her stolen gummy bears
from the gas station down the street;
she'd wink as she blew
clouds into the air and
dared me to ask how she'd do
it.

Sometimes her eyes caused my
tongue to swell and my lips to crack,
the sounds of moths flying
into Lights drove me mad
and I forgot how to speak
syllables,
but if I ever formed the words she
did not acknowledge I was there,
at all.

Maybe it was the deep guttural
growl
we had heard in the bottomless
pit your brother found
a summer ago that changed
the weather and the temperature
of the sound we stood in,
or maybe she just up
and decided it was all too much
Thin Mints and sleeping on the carpet in a too large house
or maybe it was loneliness
but she left the window open and snow had piled by the door.

I used to hope that the innocence stayed
with us the same way
her new tattoo would stay on her skin
but it melts away
when under intense heat,

I never quite got used to sleeping
under an uncomfortable blanket
of silence and questions left unasked
and wonderings of when she'd come home at last.

People told me to stop calling the number
on the door because it was going nowhere,
but the lady on the phone was
close enough to your voice that I fell asleep
listening to the
leave your message after the tone
on repeat.

Remember when you pretended to smoke cigarettes
and ate gummy bears you stole
from the corner street?
Forget the parts where you turned
to leave,
I know I was a stupid summer kid
but you were always art to me.

In Forest Park by Vivian Belle

The Carrybrowns by Jenny Kalahar

I knew the Carrybrowns
in the days when I was little
and wore flowered ankle socks
red canvas shoes with white laces gone dingy
and dresses.
And then later, when I dressed in pants like my big brothers did
to follow them up good climbing trees
or to sit straddling a creaking, fraying rope
atop our comfortable tire swing,
its rubber odor imprinting on my mind.
When I step into a tire shop
the things I did on sunny days
and even when it rained
come back to me like a rediscovered letter
from when I knew the Carrybrowns

The Carrybrowns were neat as pins, my mother said,
with a yard like a car-lot showroom,
their plants in copper bowls as big as bathtubs gone round.
The Carrybrowns were churchers
scrubbed with soap behind their ears from birth
never a stain on their white shirts during services
or after
when they all filed into the Families Eat Here
at the business end of Maple

I remember the Carrybrowns.
They lived quietly
played checkers and chess in near-silence
on their open, white-painted porch
where they could easily gaze between game moves
at the violet and cardinal flowers in their giant copper kettles,
or at the browngreen salamanders who napped
beneath a bronze frog planter
that took care of the mailbox
even when it rained

I remember that when I wanted peace and calm
I would stroll a block from home to sit on their sidewalk,
and the Carrybrowns wouldn't shoo me off
and all was cool and fine at that end of things
at that part of town
where never an argument was found
over at the Carrybrowns

But then in about nineteen eighty
Mrs. Carrybrown's father passed
and they brought her mother down from way upstate —
so far north that she had a funny accent —
and they, Mr. and Mrs. Carrybrown,
put Granny Smith in a tiny log cabin of a place
at the cleared back acre of their property

I remember the way Granny would shake and swat
her rag rugs on the steps of that cabin
each *thump* a complaint to the wind about its dust,
or a protest that the Carrybrowns' muddy-pawed schnauzer
had snuck inside to sit next to the refrigerator that hummed
and was too hot on its backside to be safe

I remember that once Granny had gotten comfortable
she started to make a change.
Soon the Carrybrown kids weren't interested in chess and checkers,
in white church shirts with nary a stain on them
and in talking quietly, mostly only when asked a question.
We kids listened to Granny's rock 'n roll records
and ate brownies with extra caramel syrup all through them with
Elvis,
vanilla ice cream with red strawberries out of a frozen can with Jerry
Lee Lewis,
and Granny's pale green bread-n-butter pickles
and grilled cheese so gooey it was halfway to sin with Little Richard
wailing on

Within a month there wasn't a quiet end of the street
as we danced in the back yard after school at the Carrybrowns.
And it turned out that Mr. and Mrs. Carrybrown were a lot happier

being free of their uptightness
the uptightness that Mr. Carrybrown had been raised on
and that Mrs. Carrybrown —
back when she was Miss Smith —
had learned to get used to if she was going to date and marry her man

I remember the freshness of the songs on those old 45 records.
I can see them drop from their held-aloft stack.
I can see the arm rotate and fall into black grooves
and we all would go crazy
eating everything, dancing away the afternoon
forgetting things like chores and homework
and fights at school
and how our parents were Republican and would just about die
if they knew we were swinging each other around and around
even when it rained in the Carrybrowns' back yard.
Even when it rained

Takeoff by Alys Caviness-Gober

Over Breakfast by Maik Strosahl

Remembering you and me
and the words spoken
over breakfast,
spread as jam on our toast.

You dreamed of flowers planted
in a backyard of your own,
and I spoke of flying off
with newly grown wings.

The memory feels warm,
of fresh coffee steam rising
into the conversations
of yester-tables.

Funny how the roses
now bloom in my garden,
while you found feathers
and freedom far away.

Even burnt bacon would taste better
peppered with your laughter –
I have not yet learned
to make breakfast just for one.

And So We Charge On by D.L. Dasher

My friends, we race on charging steeds
With soaring spirits and pounding hearts
Certain of our path, and that our deeds
Will live fore'er in the poet's arts.

But trails seldom lead where we thought we'd go
But instead to places, both harsh and low
Oh, there's better sights ahead, we know!
And so we charge on.

And as we tread an uncharted course
A friend is flung from his speeding horse
We mourn his fate but no remorse
Will stop us from charging on.

Some disappear down branching paths
Some stop, and now with doubt they ask
Is this the life to which we're tasked?
But still we charge on.

Some wish to turn back, but how?
Our previous paths have vanished now
To finish what we've begun, we vow.
We will charge on.

By The Roadside by Alys Caviness-Gober

Wishing by Alys Caviness-Gober

I think a lot about weird stuff. Like, for example, a while back I started wondering how I know stuff. Certain stuff, I mean, not the *book-larning* stuff we learn in school. I mean, I honestly don't remember the moment I understood how babies got made ~ or as some folks might say, sex stuff. It seems like I should remember that moment, right? I mean, it's a fairly significant moment in a child's life, isn't it? A light-bulb moment where all the secretive hush-hush, *nice little girls don't talk about that stuff*, and *good girls don't* scenarios of childhood crash into knowledge that's clear and, for some kids, rather terrifying. A head-tilting-up-then-down-in-a-nod-of-understanding-as-eyes-widen-eyebrows-raise-mouth-opens-in-perfect-circle *OH* moment of clarity and awareness, right?

Well, looking back over my 55 years of life on this planet, I just don't remember any such moment. I do remember knowing that you don't talk about how babies are made or toilet stuff or the body parts that your underwear covers. Heck, you don't even mention underwear! I remember knowing, just knowing ~ that all those things are *private*. I don't remember being *told* all that stuff is private, and I don't remember being told *not* to talk about all that stuff. It's more like I don't remember a time that I didn't just *know* that all that stuff was, like, seriously unmentionable, quite simply off the table insofar as discussion was concerned.

Which makes me wonder, how'd I learn all that stuff if I don't remember learning all that stuff?? I wish I knew! But that's wish for another day. Today's wish is about stuff I *do* remember learning. It's stuff you learn the hard way most of the time. It's stuff in the category of: *man, I wish I knew then what I know now*.

I wish I knew when I was five years old that: my elder sister isn't the boss of me. I wish I knew then that there'd come a day when, after a lifetime of dealing with narcissism and sociopathic lies and machinations, I'd cease to allow her in my life. I wish I knew then what I know now: *it feels good to feel like I never even had a sister*.

I wish I knew when I was ten years old that: fear is more powerful than love because then I would've known that moving away doesn't help. Nowhere in this country is a place that is free of racism and intolerance, because racism and intolerance are taught generation to generation with tools of fear and hatred. Fear of "other" makes us hate "other," right? I wish I knew then that what I know now: the *Constitution* may separate Church and State and guarantee Life Liberty and the Pursuit of Happiness to all, Lincoln may have freed the slaves, the Greatest Generation may have fought and died to protect us from Fascism, and Civil Rights may have had a movement, and Equal Rights for women may have had a movement, and Ryan White died whilst teaching us that science and truth are more powerful than fear and intolerance, and Christ might have preached that *Above All These Is Love*, but I wish I knew then that what I know now: *dammit the truth is that all those things sound good and did some good, but they don't mean shit in the real world, and the proof of that is that Donald Trump and Mike Pence got elected.*

I wish I knew when I was twelve years old that: the boy two rows over in class is nothing to be afraid of. I wish I knew then that the stares daggering me from under his heavy eyelids, the playground hair-pulling and chasing, and the knocking into me in the lunch line were all just his way of saying, I like you. I wish I knew then what I know now: *at any age, someone liking you is a good thing.*

I wish I knew when I was fourteen years old that: real people are more magical that the people on the screen in my beloved old Golden Age of Hollywood 1930s-40s movies. I wish I knew then what I know now: those wonderful cinematic faces, with their beautifully applied make-up and filmed in black and white or Vivid Technicolor showing off facial planes of contrasting perfection, speaking the well-written words of skilled storytellers, and moving around carefully and gloriously in amazingly designed costumes and sets that draw me in like magicians mesmerizing me, yes they may always be safe and perfect slices of escape, but their perfection and safety is marred by one simple truth: they are not actually here. They are not the LIVING BEINGS living real lives in my real world. I wish I knew then what I know now: *the real magicians are the real people, flawed and perfect all at once, who draw you into the magic circle of their protecting embrace, flawed and perfect all at once, driving you crazy with their imperfections, and mesmerizing you with the safety of their flawed-and-perfect-all-at-once love.*

I wish I knew when I was eighteen years old that: leaving for college (or anything else) doesn't have to hurt everyone so much. Me, on the cusp of growing into adulthood, getting away finally *finally* from the stifling blanket of bizarre rules and the running always running, as I approached leaving for college, as I at times I treated my parents rudely or roughly in order to "feel separate" from them, and my parents, facing the cold-sweat-inducing fears associated with releasing a precious fragile child into the oft-cruel world, may have been harsh and suffocating to said child as she prepared to leave. I wish I knew then what I know now: *growing up doesn't mean growing away.*

I wish I knew when I was twenty-two years old that: working a minimum wage 37.5-hour-a-week-no-benefits fast-food kitchen job on the midnight shift while trying to attend college classes in the daytime was GLORIOUS. It was ROCK 'N' ROLL, man! I should have treasured every ugly sad horrifying second of that crazy exhausting dead-end life. I wish I knew then what I know now: *that the struggling dirty starving time in my life then might have been the healthiest and the strongest I'd ever be physically.*

I wish I knew when I was twenty-four years old that: you should not marry someone you've only known for seven weeks. I'm going to leave that one there, as is. I mean, story for another day, right?? But then again, well, I oughta at least follow my pattern here. So here goes some exposition. If ever at any moment in your life, you're about to marry someone you've only known for seven weeks and everyone you know, everyone who loves and cares about you, is telling you in subtle and not-so-subtle ways not to do it, well goddammit LISTEN to them. Don't do it. I wish I knew then what I know now: *you should not marry someone you've only known for seven weeks.*

I wish I knew when I was thirty years old that: trust is not just something you give to another person. You also have to give it to yourself. For example, after a woman survives violence and abuse, she builds a wall. She lets in family, a few friends, maybe, but she stays behind that wall. Sometimes she has no intention of ever coming out from behind the wall, nor can she imagine ever letting anyone "new" in, because for that, she'd have to give them her trust, and that's just too damn scary to even contemplate let alone actually do. When the real right person actually does come along, and she lets him (or her) in, and she GIVES him (or her) trust like a precious object held in her outstretched hands and offered to him (or her) to treasure and protect, then it's so easy for people to smile and say, o*h wonderful, she tore down her wall and learned to trust again,* or *at last she found a man* (or woman) *who deserved her trust.* Well sure, all that's true, but giving your trust to another person doesn't do any good unless you can give your trust to yourself. Literally: you have to GIVE your own trust IN yourself TO yourself, like it's a precious object that you hold in your outstretched hands and offer to your mirrored self to treasure and protect. Then, and only then, are you whole, are you safe. I wish I knew then what I know now: *if you don't trust yourself, then it doesn't matter if you trust someone else ~ you still won't feel safe.*

I wish I knew when I was thirty-five years old that: someday I would think of these days, the busy crazy mad days of raising two kids under ten while working night and day towards Bachelors and Masters degrees and commuting and lesson-planning and researching and writing and *commuting commuting commuting* would lead me to being someone undreamed of at the time and doing things undreamed of at the time. Because of course at the time, you think the path is clear and straight, the learning will end, the *commuting commuting commuting* will end, and you KNOW exactly who you will be at the end of it and you KNOW exactly what your goals are and what the finish line looks like. I wish I knew then what I know now: *even if the commuting ends, you never get a clear and straight path, you never stop learning, and you never know who you'll be tomorrow or when and how goals will shape-shift or what any finish lines really look like.*

I wish I knew when I was forty years old that: there is nothing worse than watching your children hurt, and ~ no matter how hard you try ~ you can't save them from the hurt. Indeed, sometimes the harder you try, the worse they get hurt. There's nothing worse than that. Nothing. I wish I knew then what I know now: *if you can live through watching your children suffer, you can live through anything.*

I wish I knew when I was fifty years old: this is the last year that **both** my parents will be alive. I wish I knew then what I know now: *don't waste any opportunity to spend time with the people you love.*

I wish I knew when I was fifty-five years old that: *wait, I AM fifty-five years old. What do you suppose someday in the future I'll wish I'd known now?*

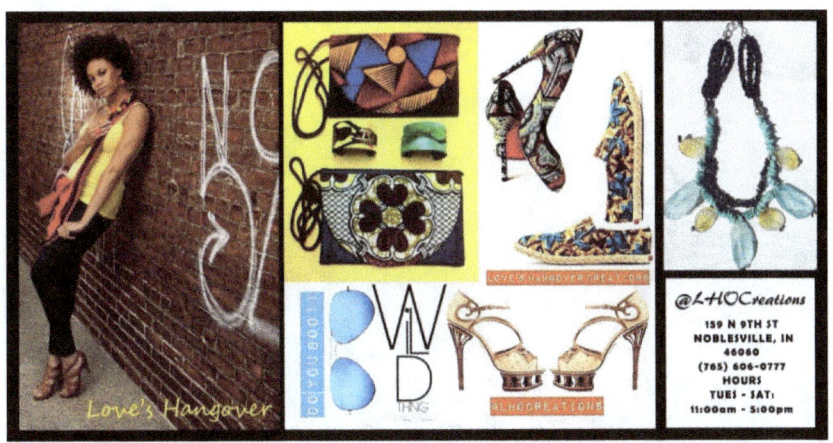

Karst Reflections by Gail Geisler
(*Red River Valley, Ha Nam, Vietnam*)

Ronnie Comes Home by Mark Wilkinson

Ronnie, my neighbor growing up in Shirley, Indiana, was ten years older than me but never treated me like the nuisance I was. He would give the neighborhood kids rides in his Dodge Hot Rod, buy us Cokes, take us to the drive-in in the bed of a pick-up truck, and, as the crowning glory of the neighborhood, bestow on each of us the nicknames that would follow us through childhood and into high school. He took that job seriously.

Sometimes the names were variations on our real names, like Tony being called Toto and Jerry being called Jewelries. Sometimes they were whatever they were. Steve was called Roper and Mick was Nubbin. Mine, however, went through a metamorphosis. I was what was called a stocky child, so Ronnie called me Chun King after a popular canned Chinese meal. He shortened that to Chunky after the candy bar, and finally to Chunk, which stuck. We were honored to have the names.

So, Ronnie was in our lives until he wasn't. In 1969, my seventh-grade year, Ronnie was drafted and went to Vietnam. The war was a distant thing to us, as were the protests against it. We watched both on TV every night. It was just another show to us. We did have a war memorial uptown that had the names of every son of Shirley that was in the military and the pictures of those killed in World War II. We looked at it often, but it had no relative significance to us kids.

I didn't worry about Ronnie in Vietnam. I was at that selfish age where I didn't worry about anyone other than myself. I know my parents worried about him because I heard them talk. They cared deeply for Ronnie. One night they whispered that Ronnie's mother Mary Alice had a nervous breakdown caused by not knowing if Ronnie was dead or alive since she had not heard from him in weeks. I was not sure what a nervous breakdown was, but I could tell by the hushed tones that it was bad.

There are times when our military truly embodies the "hurry up and wait" philosophy and there are times when it can be astonishingly efficient. This was one of the latter. The US Army was notified of Ronnie's mother's breakdown. Within two days, Ronnie was shipped from the jungle back home to Shirley, Indiana. At age 13, it was completely lost on me how significant this culture shock was on Ronnie. We were just glad to have him home.

He came over to visit my parents as we were playing basketball in the driveway. I had the best court in town.

"Hey, Ronnie." I shouted, "Want to play?"

"Sure," he said, "but I don't have any tennis shoes. They're still in Vietnam."

"That's okay," I said. "I've got some you can wear."

I gave him a pair of my rubber-cleated football shoes. He put them on and joined a team. There were nine of us, so we were playing 3-on-3 with a team waiting to play the winner. Ronnie was in the game and my team was waiting to play.

Teenagers are callow. At thirteen we think we understand the adult world and absolutely believe they know nothing of ours. We knew nothing about the war even though we watched it every night. The term PTSD was not in our lexicon. We knew nothing of fear or violent death. We knew nothing of jungles or AK 47s. We did know about firecrackers, though.

For a couple of weeks, we had been setting off illegal firecrackers that someone brought from down south. We blew up cans. We threw them at each other's feet. We set them off just because it was fun to do it. As Ronnie and his team played basketball in my driveway, we stood behind the garage with a pack of firecrackers and a lighter. As Tony flicked the lighter, I stuck the fuse in the flame. When the fuse sparked, I stepped out from behind the garage and tossed the pack of Black Cats onto the driveway. They landed behind Ronnie.

I expected the explosions to elicit some response from the players in the driveway and was rewarded when the players swore, jumped, and laughed. Except for Ronnie. He dove into the grass. As the small explosions ended, Ronnie whirled around, arms and legs outstretched in an odd crab-like stance. He was glaring at me with eyes that conveyed a clear message of fear and outrage. I knew I was in trouble.

Since then, I have heard the recorded popping of AK 47s, the assault rifle favored by the enemy in Vietnam. It sounds like firecrackers going off. Ronnie, 23 years old and two days out of the jungles of Vietnam, didn't hear firecrackers behind him. Even though he was home in Shirley, something primal and atavistic heard an AK 47 being fired a few feet away.

Ronnie was surprisingly fast. His angry eyes were bolted on me as he came out of his crouch, and he moved quickly in my direction. My reflexes were not as finely tuned. Even though I did not know exactly what I had done to make him so angry, I knew I needed to run. I had managed only two steps before he caught me. He lifted me by shirt and slammed me into the aluminum siding of the garage. His nose was pressed against mine.

"Mark," he barked, "I've known you all your life and I love you, but if you ever do something like that again, I will kick your ass all the way down the street!"

The anger went out of his eyes, replaced with a shadow of darkness that I did not recognize. He was breathing deeply as he loosened his grip and let me slide down the garage wall. No one moved, spoke, or drew a breath.

"That surprised me little," Ronnie said sheepishly. "Whose ball is it?"

We played some more basketball. Afterwards, I went inside and told my dad about the event, expecting a modicum of sympathy for his threatened son. He looked at me long and hard, and turned back to his *Indianapolis News*.

"He should have whipped your ass," he said.

I frowned as I walked away. A glimmer of self-awareness told me that I still had a lot to learn about firecrackers and war.

Peaks of Patagonia by Kirsty Crofton Geisler
(Patagonia Region, South America)

Covenant by Alys Caviness-Gober

Chosen,
she stands stoic
unable to turn
or look away.

She is bound;
victim and witness
to his destruction
and his promise.

Their bond
stands stoic
and eternal,
a covenant of love.

Witness by Alys Caviness-Gober

Rings in the Pond by Gail Mehlan

I've taken my grandchildren down to the dock to look for ducks and turtles, but nothing seems to be moving on the water today. It's very quiet. Perhaps we've scared them off with simply our presence. This does not bother the kids, though. They have found a few pebbles on the ground and are anxious to toss them into the water. They love to see them splash and the sound that they make. I, myself, love to watch the circular rings that form, and I snap a picture. It is a surprisingly unseasonably warm and sunny day. I begin to think about the start of this New Year and fresh beginnings. What is it about this year that brings me to a new beginning?

I have begun to delve into my family history again after a very long break. I was very involved with it around the year 2005, but for some reason, I put it aside for a while. Life happened! There continued to be a longing in me each time I thought about it that there was still much to be known.

Since that time, my own immediate living family has grown by leaps and bounds. Two of my children have married and brought with them their own extended families. As of today, we have 6 grandchildren ranging in age from two months to ten years. It is no less than a miracle that this much life has blessed us in such a short span of time. Life keeps marching forward.

Yesterday, we took three of our grandchildren to visit the Eiteljorg Native American museum in Indianapolis. It is a museum with information and artifacts from Native Americans who lived in Indiana, around the country, and the world. As I was looking at one of the exhibits, I read a quote from a Native American Cherokee descendent,

"Time as a river is a more Euro-American concept of time, with each event happening and passing on like a river flows downstream. Time as a pond is a more Native American concept of time with everything happening on the same surface, in the same area…and each event is a ripple on the surface."

– Dave Edmunds (Cherokee), professor, 2001

I immediately thought to myself, "Yes, for me, time flows forward like a river... That's exactly how I view it!" (A very Euro-American viewpoint!) Life keeps marching forward, no looking back, lest I turn into a pillar of salt like the wife in the story of Sodom and Gomorrah. But something stops me here. I know I could be wrong as I begin again to study and search the family history, trying to put the pieces together that weave a story of our family. I stop and think, "What if we really do ripple out from each other more like rings on a pond?" What if we don't look back, but look around us and seek the circular pattern that is made when something strikes the water?

This image haunts me. Circles all growing one inside of the other, rippling outward to a larger circle, a circle of life. I do find myself waking up at night and thinking about my ancestors being a part of my circle of life today.

As I stare out into the dark night sky, and see the many stars, I recall how God spoke to Abraham saying,

"And I will make thy seed to multiply as the stars of heaven, and will give unto thy seed all these countries; and in thy seed shall all the nations of the earth be blessed;"

– Genesis 26:4

I say a prayer to the God I know . . . and to the ancestors that can hear me.

"I want to know you! I want to know your stories, your loves, your music, and your faith! I want to KNOW you! How have your lives influenced me and mine? Reveal yourselves and your stories to me and I will record them so my own family and I don't forget!"

And then I start to think about circles, and I envision one small stone dropped in a pond and the circles continuing to grow and spread all around, yet still in the same pond. The stories of my families are numerous . . . just like the stars . . . yet somehow connected. We are connected through our DNA and through the stories I know and the ones I can only imagine.

So I take a deep breath and realize that I am just one of the many descendants of Abraham perhaps. It is a challenge of discovery for me. Where exactly did my circle in the pond begin?

As I study the different websites, I look at the random name of someone who could be an ancestor. I am looking at an unknowable face with a birthdate and a date of death. Maybe I know the names of a few of their children and perhaps even more. At the same time, I know there are clues about that person that I am missing. I so want to know. I continue to hunt for them like I'm on a mysterious family treasure hunt. The Internet is its own kind of bottomless pit, one thing leads to another on and on.

I am hoping that one day it will all start to make sense for me, that I can accept the mystery and the questions that I have to leave unanswered. I must trust that this is the beginning of a marvelous story. It's only when I realize that I am only at the beginning of this journey that I can actually sleep, trusting that the stories will be revealed to me as my research continues. The story of my families will unfold.

Somehow this circle of life image has struck a larger cord for me as I, we, face a New Year. There are so many changes that are coming quickly down the river at us like a rapid current. Our lives will be changed perhaps in ways we may not want. This can be from political changes that will undoubtedly happen in the coming weeks, or we could be blindsided by any number of different situations . . . I don't want to be a "Negative Nelly" about it and I don't want to look back either. Perhaps I just need to look around at the ripples instead of being washed away like a river.

"Bring it on!" I say to myself as I study my family tree and discover stories of families who continued to survive the concentric rings of life branching outward from Abraham to, me . . . to us.

Would I have followed my mariner husband across the ocean on a ship similar to the Mayflower to a new world with so many unknowns? Would I have survived the loss of several "Marys" as infants and still passed the beloved name on to the next female infant? How many tears were shed for those babies? Would I have survived the "revolution" of the Revolutionary War? Would I have sworn my loyalty to a newly formed government and been willing to offer up even my life to support them? Would I, or even *could* I, have continued to face life after half of my family died in an Indian massacre? Even as I think about how horrible it must have been, in looking at the history of how "we" (European settlers) took so much away from the Native Americans, somehow, I cannot carry forward any anger towards those settlers.

Would I have looked forward to a new regime when my two sons died of dysentery during the Civil War? Would I have been proud to earn a medal defending Washington DC during the Civil War when my very own brother had died in combat at Spotsylvania? Would I have carried on my life with breast cancer and two young children after my husband committed suicide with a shotgun at the start the Great Depression? These are just a few of the stories that I've discovered in reviewing my family history. These are some amazing stories of survival after losing much. And yet after all of that, my family is still here. We have survived, are surviving. We found a way to be resilient.

Madeline L'Engle in *All that was Good* writes:

"If I affirm that the universe was created by a power of love, and that all creation is good. I am not proclaiming safety. Safety was never part of the promise. Creativity, yes; safety, no. All creativity is dangerous . . . to write a story or paint a picture is to risk failure. To love someone is to risk that you may not be loved in return, or that the love will die. But love is worth the risk, and so is birth, its fulfillment."

So, I end these thoughts about beginnings with this simple thought.

No matter what the future brings or what is about to happen in this New Year. **Take the risk.**

Rachel Held Evans on her blog encourages us to:

"Finish the book. Pursue the relationship. Begin the ministry. Push the boundaries. Join the march. Write the screenplay. Do the dishes. Plant the onions. Carry the child. Roll around on the floor with your giggling toddler as if the world was even fractionally worthy of his presence."

I could add to that as well for myself, *Complete the family tree. Tell the stories.*

So I tell myself that this New Year is beginning and will be different. There will be difficulties to survive amidst the laughter and love we enjoy. I will continue to live my life and investigate my history. The sun will come up in the morning and set in the evenings. The circles of life will continue to grow and carry us outward, onward, *and* forward.

Rings In The Pond by Gail Mehlan

Strangers by John Caviness

(reflections based upon looking back at what I wrote in 2014 and 2015 in a travel blog, *Share the View: Anteil der Aussicht,* while I studied abroad in Germany.)

Last night, I spent time with friends old and also new. Waking up the morning of that day, I couldn't have guessed that my evening would include meeting the people I met. Meeting people can open your eyes to things you couldn't perhaps see before. My usual group met up happily, since we all felt as though it had been too long (five days or so). We had our fun, as we always did, but before I describe some of my experiences of the evening, I'd like to mention something I've come to notice about groups.

Groups of people go through stages, and the stages are always rather interesting to take note of as they occur. At first, there is a certain amount of mystery in the group. It's a time where slowly group norms are created, a testing of group-tolerance, and a development of core of acceptable behavior. Group rituals are established soon thereafter. Then, once the group-seed breaks the soil and sprouts, the group and its norms alter from what they once were into a whole new beast, equipped with references, sarcasm, and experimental actions that in the previous stage would have been seen as "too soon." These actions pave the way to the next stage, which I dislike greatly, since it tends to be the last stage: distancing due to false familiarity.

These sorts of dynamic group progressions are extremely volatile and interesting, sometimes fast moving or slow in nature, but the important thing to remember is that the times one has had building connections and sharing life with others more than makes up for the woes of group distancing.

My group had fun that night, and it matured along pleasantly; we were becoming more and more comfortable with each other. Our group's stages are stories for another day; today I'll write about happened after we hit my group's usual haunt, a place laughingly named *Hamburger Point*. The burgers are cheap, tasty, and right across from the train station, where normally we part ways. Rather than leaving immediately after eating our burgers, which is what we usually did, we made conversation with strangers. I spoke French, Spanish, German, and English that night, some languages better spoken than others, but all in all, I stumbled into conversations with some interesting folks who simply wanted to talk for the sake of talking.

First, there was Russian fellow, who was arrogant. Real piece of work, his name was immediately forgotten once he began talking down to the gentlemen I will mention soon. One who sits on such a high horse needn't be remembered; pride is an ugly shade on a person. The Russian had a German friend, who was more tolerable, but I only spoke with him briefly since they both were drunkenly hitting on my friend. Regardless, once they figured out where they stood in her eyes, they left.

There was a Polish-German fellow, who was kind and humble, his name was Pietrek. He asked a friend of mine for a cigarette. When my friend gave him the cigarette, Pietrek gave my friend a beer in exchange, just to return a favor. Nicely enough, he purchased one for me as well, for simply talking with him.

He said: "Good company is tough to find these days, na?" (he spoke in German, so I've translated for the sake of simplicity.)

We spoke of the terrible weather, how we all miss home, and how we respectively came to Germany. Not one of us had a bad thing to say, outside of damning the ever-present and consistent rain.

Then I met a man from Cote d'Ivoire, who was generous and talented, but regardless of all that was also without opportunity. His name was Étienne. He spoke French as his mother language, Spanish, Portuguese, Italian, and English, also. I did what I could to speak French with him at first, but later we had to go to English since the French vocabulary he used eventually blew me out of the conversation. I was surprised to learn he was homeless, since he told me that back in France he had both a degree and job, but he lost his job due to business leadership changes. He came to Germany in search of a better life, and he told me that living on the street here is safer/more comfortable than being back in his home country, out of work and homeless. He then held up his drink to me, and I held up mine to his, and we toasted to Germany. He was accompanied by his friend, Achmed, who hailed from Guinea. Achmed's story emphasized a cruelty of the world. Achmed told me a similar story of how he left a problematic home country, in search of a better life in Germany. He told me he wished to eventually become an engineer here, since he used to go to school for that back home, but he couldn't get work here or there in this field. Back home it was because there were no jobs, and here he told me no one would hire him due to his skin color. Racism isn't dead, folks, not here, and not in the States.

The question I now ask, is, what can *you* learn from a stranger?

"Be a good listener. With rapt attention, let every communication or conversation you have with your mentor, friends or even strangers be well understood." – Israelmore Ayivor

Reflections in Vietnam by Danika Geisler
(Phu Li, Vietnam)

Points by Kitty O'Doherty

Points. Everyone's giving out points these days. I seem to have collected a lot of points lately. Airline points, Verizon points, Walgreen points, AARP points, various hotel points, Kroger fuel points, and points for coffee at Speedway gas. I've tallied my known points and I have about 3,139, 967, give or take a few. My favorite earned points were the three-way split with my boyfriend and co-adventurer, Dan, for giving the correct answer (Blue Morpho butterfly) to a question posed by biologist Dagoberto Mora, during an extraordinary trip we took to Costa Rica. Dago was leading a group of eight of us on a rainforest hike and as such was educating and engaging us in a fun way by posing nature questions and assigning imaginary and random "points" for answers.

Dan and I had long prepared for this trip by reading up and familiarizing ourselves with the large variety of native species we'd hoped to see in this beautiful country. We actually scored a lot of "points" overall despite an overly competitive group member named Bob, who kept stealing answers. Bob took the exercise very seriously and was gunning for "points." He didn't trust his wife's responses, so he had no shame as he'd shout out the answers he'd overheard others quietly deliberate among themselves. Bob's ego needed points at any cost.

The first time he took an answer of ours, I was a little indignant. He had taken our solid five imaginary points for knowing what an *agouti* was. He wouldn't have known an *agouti* from a pizza topping (for the record, an *agouti* is species of rodent with kind of a squirrel head and a guinea pig butt). At some point, it just became funny watching Bob work the game.

By the end, Dan and I were headed for a "win" but a big seven points were stolen outright when once again Bob eavesdropped on our private consulting. Before we could respond to the final question, Bob yelled out the pilfered words, "Chestnut-mandibled Toucan!" for the victory in the rain forest.

Bob was thrilled to be the winner! Dan and I waited for the fallout when Bob immediately asked Dago what he would receive for winning all of the points. The biologist told him he got nothing. Bob was crushed.

"The points were . . ." Dago explained, ". . . merely for fun."

Bob turned sulky and glum. He really wanted something tangible for his point-gathering.

I imagine he has never totally recovered from that moment of learning he worked and stole points for nothing.

As we moved forward up the path, I thought I heard a White-headed Capuchin monkey giggle up high in the canopy as Bob grumbled and shuffled his feet at the unfairness of it all.

"If I Only Knew Then What I Know Now. . ." by Marlene Million
(a 2018 *NICE* entry, inspired by *The Odyssey*)

I had no idea, in my early days of marriage, that I would be facing my husband's ill health, taking over our budget and finances, and being a care-giver to my husband taking the role of provider in our retirement years. The journey for both Odysseus and Penelope parallels my life to where I am today. Odysseus's life journeyed into detours throughout Ancient Greece along the way home to Ithaca to his wife Penelope and son Telemachus. Throughout his journey, he battles nasty winds, forgets his purpose at times, faces an irresistible force in Circe, passes through an enormous whirlpool, yet wishes to be home with his beloved wife and move forward in their life together. Penelope is the long-long-suffering wife, the symbolic mother, the "ideal woman." She stays firm in her belief that her husband is alive and well.

My husband and I started our marriage after his sophomore year in college. We considered ourselves partners; I worked to put my husband through his last two years of college. I had finished attending a Junior/Business college after high school and was hired on the spot at a business in West Lafayette, Indiana. My husband finished his degree from Purdue University in business. We had a family within the next two years, Tom went into business for himself in insurance; I helped in the office as manager. When the kids became sick, my husband would let me take the day off so I could take care of our children. Tom had always taken care of the home budget, since he was a businessman and was good with figures.

Tom had open-heart surgery on Feb. 20, 2017,;he spent four months in rehab. We had been retired for several years at the time. I had to step into the role of household manager – handling the budget and finances at home and visiting him in rehab every day. At first, my task seemed daunting, as I was not familiar with the budget, working with figures, or handling expenses. This was Tom's job, since he handled the business and home finances all our married life! Yet, day by day, I settled not a routine, making out a budget, handling whatever came my way, and I kept the checkbook balanced! Whew!
Then Tom fell and fractured his hip in September of 2017. I kept moving forward through his many months of therapy, doctor visits, another small surgery to put in a pacemaker/defibrillator, and finally home after months of rehab from hip surgery. He is still recovering.

"For richer, for poorer, in sickness and in health, to love and to cherish . . ."

Tom and I celebrated our 50th wedding anniversary on August 17, 2018! When my husband needed to me to take charge, I stayed loyal to the task, praying with deep faith that kept me believing in Tom's recovery. My life has echoed Penelope's day-to-day strength, her perseverance, and faith that Odysseus would return to her. Odysseys' journey home is just like Tom's continued journey returning to health every day. Despite our roles being reversed, I have maintained order in our household. Both Tom and I had trials, were tested, and came out triumphant in our journey as husband and wife. Although I didn't know at the beginning of our marriage that our roles would be reversed, everything has turned out fine . . . to a happy ending!

Power to the People by Gail Geisler
(Hanoi, Vietnam 2018)

Perito Moreno Glacier by Kirsty Crofton Geisler
(Santa Cruz Province, Argentina)

Dammit by David Allen

Sitting here
drinking coffee,
scarfing down
a cheese Danish,
waiting for the atheists
to arrive.
A movie night
with the Okinawa
Freethought Society,
gonna watch a flick
about how religion's
"The Root of All Evil,"
by Richard Dawkins.
But it's already 8 p.m.
and no one's
showed up yet.

Goddamit!
Where the hell
 are they?

(If I knew I'd be alone
I'd have just stayed home)

Bonnie Scotland by Kirsty Crofton Geisler

Amsterdam by John Caviness

(reflections based upon looking back at what I wrote in 2014 and 2015 in a travel blog, *Share the View: Anteil der Aussicht,* while I studied abroad in Germany.)

Amsterdam is one of the biggest tourist attractions that I've heard about for much of my life, and as I traveled there, I was eager to see in person all that I had heard and read about: what could be better than to visit a city that was a combination of history (I'm here to learn, after all), a new (to me) culture, and infamous freedoms? I spent seven hours there, and six hours just getting there. I ended up getting a little sick due to the weather, but besides that, here was my experience . . .

I saw the Anne Frank house, and even though I didn't go inside, to say it is a haunting experience to just see it from the outside puts it mildly. One cannot *truly* imagine her life in that house, even after reading her eloquent journal. I plan to visit Auschwitz in the Spring and being in front of this historic spot was like a first leg in that upcoming journey.

Amsterdam is full of many beautiful old buildings, and scattered amongst them are the silly French Fry stands. Within the first hour of my visit, I saw four in one place, four different companies selling the same product: French Fries in cones drenched in either mayonnaise or ketchup. Of course, I saw the Red Light district. One of the infamous freedoms, right? Since the 16th Century, prostitution in Amsterdam has been regulated. In 1810, Napoleon further regulated prostitution in the Netherlands to protect his army from venereal diseases: prostitutes had to register, and they had to have mandatory medical examinations. Registered prostitutes were given a red card, acted as a work permit. During the 19th century, sexual morals became stricter, and there arose a movement against regulated prostitution; in 1911, owning brothels, adult movie theaters, and escort companies was prohibited by law, but prostitution itself was not illegal.

During the second half of the twentieth century, prostitution and brothels were pretty much condoned and tolerated by the authorities. The police rarely made prostitution-related arrests, unless public order was at stake, or if they could prove human trafficking. The reasoning behind this *gedoogbeleid* (policy of tolerance) was "harm reduction." Basically, the idea was that the best way to "protect the women" was to tolerate the illegal activity of prostitution. Harm reduction policy is not limited to prostitution; it has been and still is also applied to illegal drugs. Prostitution was defined as a legal profession in 1988, and owning brothels, adult movie theaters, and escort companies became legal in 2000. Well, anyway, I saw the Red Light district briefly, because what I saw disgusted me: nothing makes you dislike a place more than seeing institutionalized gender exploitation within the first hour.

Speaking of the infamous freedoms, a little history about cannabis and coffeeshops. In 1953, cannabis (marijuana) was made illegal in the Netherlands; prior to that, laws just prohibited its import and export. In 1972, the Dutch government divided drugs into two categories: more- and less-dangerous, with cannabis being in the less-dangerous category. The possession of 30 grams or less was made a misdemeanor. That's pretty much when the mythology Amsterdam's legalized marijuana started. It isn't 100% legal, but cannabis has been openly sold for "recreational use" in certain "coffeeshops" since 1976, and possession of up to 5 grams for personal use is actually legal (but the police can confiscate it, which often happens in car checks near the borders).

First-time visitors to Amsterdam can get confused by the terms used for different establishments: a *koffiehuis* (coffee house) differs from a *café* (casual restaurant or bar), but a licensed seller of cannabis products is always referred to as a "coffeeshop." Just look for a green and white sticker in the window: that sticker means the owner holds a license, designating the establishment as a coffeeshop. Now, such coffee shops *do not* sell alcohol, because in 2007, Dutch laws dictated that a shop may sell either alcohol or cannabis products but not both. Weird, right?

Anyway, other types of cannabis sales and transportation are illegal, although the harm reduction approach toward cannabis has been in effect pretty much forever.

Naturally, I went into some coffeeshops, just to see if they even sold coffee, which most of them didn't. I also saw the "coffee drinkers," in their clouded rooms, all stifling their laughter. Same of them clearly had enjoyed a few too many *spacecakes*, which are sweet cakes baked with marijuana in them. Funnily enough, I witnessed a tourist smoke a cigarette at an outdoor coffeeshop, with joints being smoked all around him: he was asked to leave since he was smoking tobacco.

Amsterdam is strange, I think, and has a special way of functioning. I saw red-eyed folk on the streets, devouring French Fries doused in ketchup or mayonnaise, with fat policemen sitting on the hood of their cars, exchanging jokes in Dutch. There were many bikers with joints hanging out of their mouths, tourists wearing silly hats with *AMSTERDAM* plastered upon them. There are surprising cleaner streets than most towns I've been to up until this day. Beyond seeing easily 1000 headshops each equipped with all the gear a stoner could need and more, I saw psychedelic mushrooms for sale in the windows of some businesses; I saw purchasers promptly eat them while standing just around the corner of the very business that sold them.

There are, for the tourist, some unbelievable sights to see in Amsterdam, from ladies dancing barely clothed in windows to stoners and mushroom-eaters partaking openly of their drugs of choice to more cheese stores than I think a town can really justify having, without creating a cheese surplus. I wandered around the town for seven hours, occasionally talking to people, but more often than not, I spent the time just marveling at the foreignness of Amsterdam. I do not think I will go back, but at least I can say I went.

"Some tourists think Amsterdam is a city of sin, but in truth it is a city of freedom. And in freedom, most people find sin." – John Green

She's Got The World At Her Fingertips by Leslie Ober

The World is at Her Fingertips by Leslie Ober

The world is at her fingertips.
At least that's what they say.
The world is at her fingertips.
And change is on the way.
Big dreams upon the horizon;
Bigger fears buried within.
The world is at her fingertips.
And she's not giving in.
Her feet are set on solid ground;
Running faster than before.
The world is at her fingertips.
Adventure's knocking at her door.
Will she rise to the occasion?
Or will she stumble there and fall?
The world is at her fingertips.
Awaiting the answer to her call.
She takes a breath and leap of faith;
Trusting that this is right.
The world is at her fingertips.
This little bird has taken flight.
The world is at her fingertips.
At least that's what they say.
The world is at her fingertips.
And change is on the way.

Hints from Heloise by Kitty O'Doherty

When I was really young and learning to read, the most regular reading sources in my house were the daily paper and the telephone book, and I loved them both.

It was in the early 1960s and I was not yet understanding the *Indianapolis Star* headlines pertaining to the Vietnam war and local business concerns, so my favorite parts of the paper were the comics, *Dear Abby*, and *Hints from Heloise*.

I didn't much understand a lot of the issues in *Dear Abby*, but it gave an interesting glimpse into adult troubles. Your husband came home with lipstick on his collar? Hmmm. My eight-year-old self would offer that your husband just needs to wash his shirt. I believe that Tide stuff I see on TV would help him knock that stain out. Seemed like a dopey question to me. But in *Hints from Heloise*, there was a gold mine of more relatable stuff, and they even printed letters from kids, who always signed off with their age, "Signed, Debbie, age 12." The 12-year-olds were really good. They could write and they had enough life experience to be able to give credible household advice to adults. I admired them greatly and had hoped one day to have my own fabulous hint to contribute.

The only thing that bugged me about Heloise was that most of her column was made up of hints sent in by readers, despite being titled, *Hints from Heloise*. She would reply to each, and be genuinely warm and folksy, but in reality most hints came from her readers. It's goofy, but I was a very literal child and remember feeling annoyed that the title claimed to have hints FROM her, when clearly they were the ideas of others. I wrestled with the ethics of that nearly every time I read her column until I was about, well, no, actually I never did reconcile that. But I eventually toned down my obsession with the semantics so I could enjoy baking tips from Carol in Albuquerque, a grease stain removal idea from Fran in Des Moines, or an oven-cleaning solution from Nancy in Ashtabula.

Unfortunately, I never ended up contributing a hint. I was sad when Heloise passed away because she almost seemed like an aunt that you never saw but really liked. She certainly should get credit for being the seedling that led to Pinterest and all of today's lifestyle blogs. Her invitation for people to write in and offer their own experience has morphed exponentially and turned into a social phenomenon. Everyone is always looking for a better way, a kind of eureka moment in everyday life that they can share. Her daughter has carried on the column and deals with modern situations, such as burnt popcorn smell in microwaves and what to do when your cell phone falls in the bath, but "my" Heloise will always be her beloved mom talking to us "gals."

Future Pearl by Danika Geisler
(taken at a cultured pearl farm on Halong Bay, Vietnam)

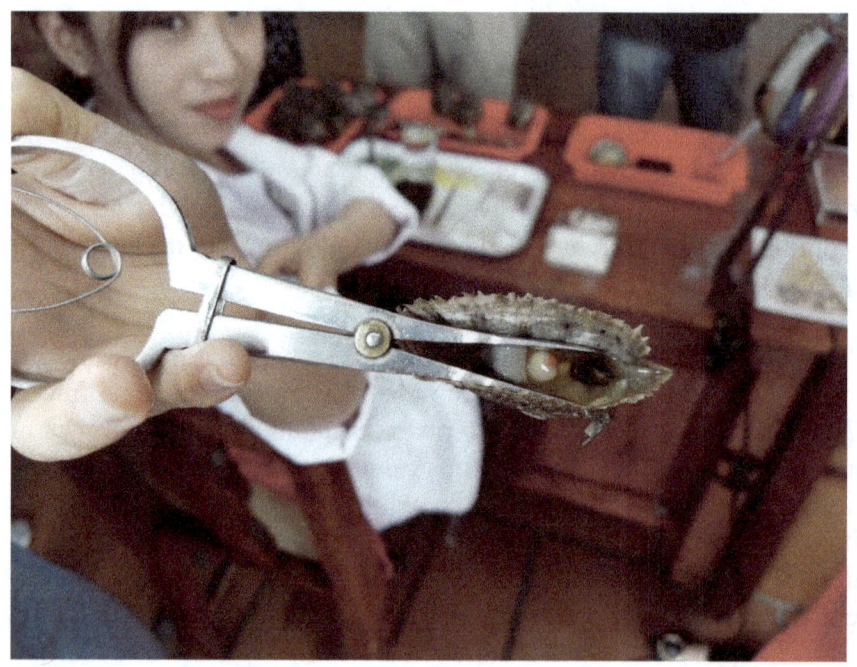

End Notes about Polk Street, Grasshoppers, and *Logan Street Sanctuary, Inc.*

Old Mill & Grain Elevator, 8th Street, Noblesville, Indiana
photograph by Alys Caviness-Gober

The Polk Street Review book is named in honor of a street that is significant to Noblesville. In 1823, when Noblesville was laid out, one of the main routes through town was named after William Connor's partner, Josiah Polk. It's the north/south road now named 8th Street, the one with a railroad track running alongside and down the middle of it. Those tracks and the trains that ran on them, until just a few years ago, are unfortunately under threat from development plans now. Noblesville may see these heritage railway train tracks vanish if the developers have their way, but Noblesville residents who honor and celebrate their city's history hope not. They believe that Noblesville can retain the historic small-town qualities that make it unique from its neighbors, and still honor its history as a place of growth and development. Certain areas, certain landmarks, and certain streets play a big part in that vision. The railroad tracks in and along Noblesville's old Polk Street are a good example of what shaped Noblesville in the past, and what makes Noblesville still feel special today.

In the early days of Noblesville's history, Polk Street was a busy road:

the north end was where mills were located, and it was lined along its southern stretch with the old courthouse, bars, liveries, hotels, homes, and other buildings of industry. At some point, Polk Street/8th Street became the dividing line between white-collar and blue-collar neighborhoods, white and African-American neighborhoods, residential and industrial areas, and high ground *versus* the flood plain. Over time, those distinctions became so ingrained that people didn't really mentioned them much, and now most folks see 8th Street as exactly what it originally was: a main route through town.

The busy street, like history itself, can be taken for granted, but it represents the history of Noblesville, her businesses, and the generations of people who have lived here. *The Polk Street Review*'s purpose is to capture and celebrate that history and the people who live and work here (past and present!) in submissions of prose, poetry, song lyrics, and images. We have one rule for submissions to the book: either the subject matter in a submission or the submitter must have a connection to Noblesville.

You may have heard us refer to our *The Polk Street Review* contributors as "grasshoppers" and to the people who quietly support them as "ants." These insect references are taken from Aesop's fable, *The Ant & The Grasshopper*. Grasshoppers are the dreamers, the creatives: the artists, writers, and musicians among us. Ants are the ones who support them: the hardworking loved ones toiling away in the background, the ones who handle the realities of life. Grasshoppers create that which inspires, that which feeds the soul; ants create that which feeds the body. The world needs both ants and grasshoppers, so cheers to both!

Logan Street Sanctuary, Inc. is a 501(c)(3) nonprofit cultural arts organization that rents space at 1274 Logan Street in Noblesville for our diverse arts and music programming. Our 501(c)(3) is run by a small band of dedicated people that make up our all-volunteer Board. Perhaps some would call us dreamers, but we work hard to fulfill our LSS mission!

Logan Street Sanctuary, Inc.'s mission is to promote a greater awareness of and encouragement for Creative Arts in Hamilton County and beyond; to provide music, literature, and arts education, events, and exhibitions, which meet the interests of the community in general, and to encourage music, literature, and art by all in the community by providing exhibits, events, and venue space for exhibits, events, and educational classes and workshops. *Logan Street Sanctuary, Inc.* hopes to establish high aesthetic standards and to cooperate with, and promote membership in, other similar organizations. Thank you to our 2019 Board members for all their hard work!

2019 LSS Board Officers

President: Mike Stewart
Treasurer: Joyce Perry
Secretary; Programming/Events; Marketing & Public Relations; Development; Concert Bookings; Rentals; Membership:
Alys Caviness-Gober
Programming/Events; Marketing & Public Relations:
Sarah E. Morin-Wilson
VOR/Operations: Cris Gober
Music Outreach & Special Programming: Steve VandeWater
Hospitality/Kitchen Manager: Emily Wasonga
Theatre Outreach: Dr. Paul "Spike" Morin-Wilson
Board Member(s) At-Large: Juliana Jones

2019 The Polk Street Review Awards

Award of Merit (*Best in Book*)
Miss Betty Boop Has Now Retired by Jenny Kalahar

Prose Category

First Prize
A Difficult Life by Vivian Belle

Second Prize
Ronnie Comes Home by Mark Wilkinson

Third Prize
Joey Walnuts' Demise by Kitty O'Doherty

Honorable Mention
Belles Lettres by Deborah Petersen

Honorable Mention
What I Could Have Been by Leslie Ober

Honorable Mention
The First Time by Jo Mader

Poetry/Song Lyrics Category

First Prize
Four Metaphors by Celeste Williams

Second Prize
Frayed Jeans, Flannel Shirts by Sam Watermeier

Third Prize
To The Mother Rabbit Who Lives Under Our Deck by Bonita Cox
Searle

Honorable Mention
Summer of '17 by Maren Thornbury

Honorable Mention
Obey All Traffic Laws by Jess Coovert

Honorable Mention
The Storm Demands by Nancy Simmonds

Images Category

First Prize
Future Pearl by Danika Geisler (photograph)

Second Prize
The Grass Is Always Greener by Leslie Ober (painting)

Third Prize
If I Knew Then by Gail Mehlan

Honorable Mention
Collison by Jansen Sovich (fractal)

Honorable Mention
Power To The People by Gail Geisler (photograph)

Honorable Mention
Bonnie Scotland by Kirsty Crofton Geisler (photograph)

Special Awards

Special Award ~ *Mama's Homemade*
(Kelli Ray Yates & Kat Wedmore)

Mama's Homemade receives a *Special Award* because we love to celebrate our contributors who take risks, branch out, and/or try something new (to them). While Kelli has been a singer, musical performer, writer of prose, and guest presenter at past book launches of *The Polk Street Review*, she and the other half of *Mama's Homemade*, Kat Wedmore, took a risk when they ventured into new territory in 2018 as a songwriting partners and performers. We hope this award assures them that we are glad they took the risk, and we like what they're doing!

Special Award ~ Bryony Stanger

Bryony receives a *Special Award* because we love to celebrate first-time contributors who offer art forms that are unusual, cutting edge, or not the "norm" for submissions to our publication. We also like to recognize younger talent whenever we can, because we believe the communities and the arts can sometimes overlook the vision of youth. Bryon is young, her artistic vision and techniques are both cutting edge and unique, and she is a newcomer to both Noblesville and *The Polk Street Review*. We hope this award makes her feel welcome!

Special Award ~ Lesley Haflich

Lesley Haflich receives a *Special Award* because her portrait series celebrates some of Noblesville's influential women and includes information about the women that reflects their careers and personal lives in a way that fits in with the goals of *The Polk Street Review*. The sheer scope of her project – 29 portraits! – is deserving of recognition, and it is proof that Lesley herself is an artist who is willing to try something new in her artistic endeavors.

Contributor Biographies

David Allen is a retired journalist and published poet with two books, *The Story So Far* and *(more)*, both available at Amazon.com. He is the Vice President and contest director of the Poetry Society of Indiana, host of Open Mic Poetry Nights in Anderson, and a member of the Noble Poets and the Last Stanza Society in Elwood. Visit his blog at www.davidallenpoet.net.

Arlene Barker moved to Hamilton County from her native Chicago in 1973 and has lived just north of Conner Prairie since 1978. She taught in Hamilton Southeastern Schools, and worked at Conner Prairie for 12 years. After retirement, she revived her life-long interest in writing through the Indianapolis Writing Center. She lives in the woods with her husband, mother, and dog, Penny. Besides writing, she enjoys reading, gardening, yoga, the Cubs, and traveling to visit her children out West.

Vivian Belle lives in Noblesville. She is enjoys traveling and writing.

Alys Caviness-Gober is a disabled anthropologist, artist, and writer. She taught Anthropology and Women's Studies for several years and was a PhD candidate in Applied Linguistics at BSU until her disabilities worsened. In 2010, she formed *Sacred Heart of the Rose*, a non-denominational 501(c)(3) nonprofit spiritual organization. In 2011, she began selling artwork (*Creative Expressions Arts*) and was juried in both photography and 2D categories into the Hamilton County Artists' Association, where she served on the Board for six years. Alys and author Sarah E. Morin co-founded *NICE* (*Noblesville Interdisciplinary Creativity Expo*), now in its 5th year. In 2014, Alys founded *Logan Street Sanctuary, Inc*. She edits and publishes *The Polk Street Review*. Alys is a FY2017 Indiana Arts Commission *Individual Artist Project* Grant Award recipient, for which she created a series of paintings expressing life with hidden disabilities. In 2018, Alys began writing film reviews as a guest contributor to *Midwest Film Journal*. Alys' artwork, photographs, prose, and poetry have received national and international recognition. She lives in Noblesville with her husband, Cris Gober. Alys accepts commissions, so contact her at alys@creativeexpressionsarts.com.

Jim Caviness graduated from Noblesville High School, the United States Naval Academy, and received his medical degree from the Uniformed Services University of the Health Sciences in Bethesda, Maryland. In 2016, "Commander Doctor Jim" (as he is affectionately called by his sister, Alys) retired from the Navy after almost thirty years of service. Jim continues his medical career in California, where he lives with his wife Andrea and their two sons, Jimmy and Phillip.

John Caviness grew up in Noblesville, graduating from Noblesville High School. He received his Bachelor of Arts in Foreign Languages (German Studies) and his Master of Science from the Center for Communication and Information Sciences (CICS) at Ball State University. John loves to fix problems, ease frustration and optimize quality of life while working with technology. John started his career at KSM Consulting the same week he graduated from CICS in 2018, working to help the company and their clients thrive in the modern technology landscape. As a consultant, John joined KSMc's Team 2, tasked with troubleshooting technology problems large and small in industry spaces such as healthcare, construction, storage, paper, machinery, food, landscaping, real estate, religious organization and research companies. At KSMc, John fearlessly problem solves for his clients, especially in times of uncertainty. John has been a male ally to women throughout his life and hopes he can help both men and women work together better in the technology space. KSMc is always looking for new clients, so feel free to contact John any time with your technology questions, at jacaviness@ksmconsulting.com.

Jess Coovert grew up in Noblesville all of her life, if you discount the few collective months she spent in the South with her mom's family. Writing has always been something she enjoys, as she's an avid reader. More often than not, Jess wasn't able to find books with plots she wanted to read, so she took to writing them herself. The inspiration for Jess' poem in this anthology came from the few weeks her mom spent trying to teach her to drive and parallel park through downtown Noblesville, an experience that resulted in a few almost-accidents; thankfully Jess didn't hit anything except for a squirrel.

W.B. (William Benjamin) Cornwell is an award-winning poet, novelist, genealogy blogger, and one half of the writing team known as Storm Sandlin. Since 2014, he has been published in over a dozen books. In 2016, he and his cousin A.N. Williams co-ran the campaign for Elwood, Indiana's Poetry Month. He is also a featured writer for Goodkin.org. He is currently working on a slew of writing projects, including various charity publications, to which he is loaning his voice as a co-author, and he is dabbling in screenplays.

Mary A. Couch, a Past Premier Poet for the Poetry Society of Indiana, resides in Noblesville, and learned the art of poetry from her mother, and two grandmothers who were storytellers and artists. Her poems show hints of Celtic heritage revealing the spirits in nature and oneness of the universe in her new book, *Hoosier Haiku: Poetic Snippets from the Heartland,* as well as in *Poetic Nature in the Hoosierland, Twin Muses: Art & Poetry, An Evening with the Writing Muse, The Polk Street Review,* and *Poetry and Paint.*

Rachel Cox grew up in Noblesville and is a student at Indiana University-Purdue University Indianapolis (IUPUI), with a major in Writing & Literacy and a minor in History. After graduation she plans to go into the publishing business. She recently started working in the University Writing Center at IUPUI, and has the wonderful opportunity to work with other writers on writing! A connoisseur of mockumentaries and intrusive thoughts, she enjoys strong black tea and distrusts anyone who doesn't like cats.

D.L. Dasher is a former automotive engineer living in somewhere in the woods in central Indiana. He now writes and illustrates children's books as well as poems and short stories for adults.

Jerry Dreesen is a haiku poet and self-taught artist, who has been writing poetry and prose for more than forty years. He enjoys experimenting with various genres including *haiku, tanka, haibun,* and other short form Japanese poetry, as well as short stories and prose. He is a past *haiga* editor for *Simply Haiku,* an on-line *haiku* journal. Jerry has self-published a *haiku* chapbook, *Forgotten Promises.* He loves to challenge himself in a variety of mediums and styles including acrylic, watercolor, pastel, and linocut printing. Jerry also experiments with clay sculpture and enjoys combining poetry and various kinds of art. Jerry's poetry, prose, and art has been published in several online and print journals. Jerry has exhibited his art in various local art shows and exhibitions and has sold work throughout the United States, Canada, Great Britain, Europe, and Japan. He accepts commissions: jerrydreesen@yahoo.com.

Al Geisler has been a Noblesville resident since 1987. He is a retired Lilly mechanical engineer. Al says, *If I knew then what I know now, I would have restored the retired tractor years ago.*

Danika Geisler was born and raised in Noblesville. She attended Indiana University and now lives and works in Indianapolis. Travel is a favorite hobby of Danika's, as shown by her submissions this year of some of her photos from her travels.

Gail Geisler has ridden a bike from Colorado to Banff, worked on a kibbutz in Israel, backpacked in Alaska, climbed Mt. Kilimanjaro, biked the Cabot Trail in Nova Scotia, and trekked the Tour du Mt Blanc. In between, she worked as a shoe salesman, maid, bartender, grapefruit picker, waitress, packaging engineer, and marketing director. Gail is now a culinary student, plotting her next adventure.

Kirsty Crofton Geisler is married to Noblesville native Jesse Geisler. The couple met at Purdue University both studying engineering. They now live in southern California and love to travel the world together.

John Gilmore was born in Bloomington, Indiana. John's parents moved to Noblesville at the start of his 7th grade year. He has been here ever since. A longtime former employee of the Noblesville Post Office, he now spends his time playing guitar, fiddle, mandolin, writing songs, and chasing a couple of rowdy Rottweilers around his house and four acres.

Lesley Haflich has had a passion for art from a young age. She received her Bachelor of Fine Arts from Purdue University. After working as an art director for an advertising agency and sign company, she began oil painting about twelve years ago; she's never looked back. She learned a lot by painting with a group of women in the Hamilton County Artists' Association and by taking workshops from nationally known artists. She's been an artist member at CCA Gallery in Carmel for seven years and regularly sells paintings at Penrod Art Fair. Her paintings are part of public collections such as the Indianapolis Symphony, Columbia Club, Indianapolis Sailing Club, Conner Prairie, Flanner and Buchanan Mortuary, Jackson Lewis Law Firm, Linet Americas, and the Noblesville Mayor's Office. In October 2018 Lesley's portrait series, *The Women of Noblesville,* was exhibited in the Stephenson House at Nickel Plate Arts, 107 S. 8th Street, where Lesley has been an artist-in-residence for six years.

Patty Hunter has been writing for 30 years. In the mid-1980s, she was a freelance poet, and in the late 1990s, she also freelanced as a Gospel lyricist. Patty also does children's songs, world lyrics, and some spoken word songs. For the past 12 years, she's written lyrics for singers and has over eight songs done by songwriters/singers around the world. Recently, she wrote a poem called, *Two Little Owls,* and singer/composer Matt Gerber composed music to accompany it and recorded it. The song became a single, and the poem is in this edition of *The Polk Street Review.* Patty is originally from Toronto, in Ontario, Canada, has predominantly Celtic and Bavarian ancestry, with additional ancestors from several countries throughout Europe. Patty and her husband, Bob, now live in the United States; they have been away from Toronto for 24 years and there are times they do miss their hometown. Nine years ago, Patty became a TV Producer/Hostess of the show called, *Patty's Page.* She has 450 shows under her belt and is planning to continue for the next few years.

Jenny Kalahar is a used & rare bookseller in Elwood with her husband, Patrick. She is the author of four novels, a collection of poetry, a children's story/poetry book, an anthology of magazine columns, and a children's picture book. Jenny is on the executive board of the Poetry Society of Indiana and is their publisher, she helms Last Stanza Poetry Association, and has begun work as the president of the Youth Poetry Society of Indiana. She was twice nominated for a Pushcart Prize in poetry. Jenny has been published in the National Federation of State Poetry Societies' annual prize-winning anthology, *Encore,* in *The Poets of Madison County, Words and Other Wild Things, The Polk Street Review, Bards Against Hunger, Diamonds, Indiana Voice Journal, Tipton Poetry Journal, Trillium,* and in newspapers. She is the humor columnist for *Tails Magazine.*

Bill Kenley is a co-founder of the original *The Polk Street Review* (2011-2014) and is the author of *High School Runner (Freshman)*. One of three finalists for Emerging Author in last year's Eugene and Marilyn Glick's Indiana Authors' Awards, he's currently working on a collection of short stories. An award-winning high school English teacher of twenty-three years at Noblesville High School, he's also an avid runner, coach, and father.

Jo Mader's work has appeared in previous editions of *The Polk Street Review*. A native of Cleveland, Jo and husband John have lived in Noblesville for over 10 years. This year's entry is a memory from 1968 when John was in Vietnam and Jo and their three daughters were living in August, Georgia.

Mama's Homemade (Kelli Ray Yates and Kathleen "Kat" Wedmore) is a dynamic female singer-songwriter duo. Both Kat and Kelli have been playing music most of their adult lives. Kelli was a member of *Noble Roots* for five years, bringing her powerful and soulful voice to central Indiana and beyond. Kat's been playing guitar for nearly twenty years; she's been in several bands including *Sounds of Cicadas* and *The Squares*. Kat and Kelli met in 2017 and immediately clicked. Beginning in 2018, they began to write their own music and stepped out of the comfort zone of the living room and onto the stage.

Gail Mehlan is a retired Bilingual/ESL teacher originally from the Chicago suburbs. She and her husband moved to the area a few years ago to be closer to our grandchildren. They have many ties to Noblesville as they shop, volunteer, worship, and have family that lives and works in the community. Gail spends her time volunteering at Roots of Life Community, Little Angel Gowns, and the local schools where her grandchildren attend school. She loves to write, paint, sew, do creative lettering, and play with her grandchildren! Gail and her husband love their life on the Morse Reservoir and hope to be here and part of this community for many years to come.

Marlene Million is a member of Noble Poets, Noble Writers Group, Poetry Society of Indiana, National Fed. of State Societies, Inc., has an Associate in English, and had a poem on display at Indianapolis Arts Garden in February 2013. She has been published in a variety of chapbooks, journals, and books. Marlene is a retired State Farm Ins.

secretary, and a grandmother of four. She is currently working on a chapbook of her poetry.

Sarah E. Morin serves as a kidwrangler at Conner Prairie, a history museum in Fishers, Indiana. She writes and performs unruly fairy tales and poems and is a regular performer at Fairyville at Nickel Plate Arts. She has published two books, *Waking Beauty (*a Christian fantasy novel based on Sleeping Beauty) and *Rapunzel the Hairbrained,* a children's picture book that forms the basis of a workshop to build girls' self-esteem. Sarah E. is a state officer of Poetry Society of Indiana and co-founder of *NICE* (Noblesville Interdisciplinary Creativity Expo), which is in its 5th year in 2019. She loved the years she spent living above the Clock Shop in Noblesville, and still remains engaged in the downtown scene through Noble Poets. (New poets welcome – 3rd Tuesday of each month at 6:30pm at Noble Coffee and Tea Co.) When she grows up she wants to be a child prodigy. Visit her at sarahemorin.com.

Paul "Spike" Morin-Wilson is a professional director, actor, playwright, translator, and scholar. He holds a PhD in Theatre, with an emphasis in directing, actor training, children's theatre, and drama-for-literacy. He was the Director of the Kokomo Summer Drama Camp for nineteen years, coaching over 1,000 students, many of whom have gone on to successful careers in professional theatre. He is a former teaching fellow for the Miami University Department of Theatre and the University of Pittsburgh Dept. of Theatre Arts, and a theatre professor for Ivy Tech Community College. He has 30 years of experience in the theatre, has directed over 60 productions, and is the Artistic Director of Page & Stage Theatre Co., which teaches theatre-for-literacy through workshops, a summer camp, and soon, full-length productions.

Crystal Morrison is an aviator by day and a writer by night. She's contributed to several editions of *The Polk Street Review*. Her genres of choice include children's literature and mysteries. The first book in her *Adventures in Kibbletown* series will be released in 2019. Passionate about the writing community, she leads a thriving local writers' group. Crystal resides in Noblesville with her husband and small petting zoo comprised of three dogs and three cats.

Leslie Ober is a long-time Noblesville resident. She is a homeschooling mother of six children and spends what little free time she has painting, dabbling in photography, and writing.

Kitty O'Doherty is a resident of Old Town Noblesville, having moved here in 2016 to share in the lives of her three grandchildren, Elizabeth, Lydia, and Seth. In addition to writing stories and revving up the children with ice cream and root beer, she also enjoys photographing insects and animals, and has previously exhibited some photographs at the Hamilton County Artists' Association's *Birdie Gallery* in Noblesville. Surprisingly, this grandmother has also worked a number of years as a crew member for an amateur sport car team with her racer boyfriend, Dan. Content with general duties of driver support, spotter, strategy consultant, parts runner, and tire and equipment manager, she has no plans to get behind the wheel. Ever.

Some of you may already know **Deborah Petersen** as an educator, because for decades she taught middle and high school students, and she was a Composition professor at some local colleges as well. Some of you may know her as the current President of the Poetry Society of Indiana, as well as a Poetry Contest judge for national and state contests. Some avid readers among you may know her for her works: in 2018, she was the editor and contributor to three poetry anthologies and was a featured poet in the *Indiana Voice Journal*. It is no secret to anyone who knows Deborah that she is the living epitome of "a Word Junkie." What first influenced Deborah as a poet were the prayers of her childhood. Later, she was influenced by the complexity and cadence of William Shakespeare's works. The most recent years have moved her with the writings of the Persian Poet and Sufi Mystic, Rumi, and by the Japanese Haiku Master, Basho. As artists, Deborah believes we are mere conduits. When she is in the moment of being a conduit, she finds herself in an omniscience, a moment of vastness and grace, a connection to a universal wisdom and discerning perception.

Lawrence "Rick" Phillips lives with his wife Sheryl in Noblesville, Indiana. Rick and Sheryl married in 1977; they are blessed with two sons and three wonderful grandchildren. Rick was diagnosed with type 1 diabetes in 1974. In 2014 Rick was diagnosed with Rheumatoid Arthritis, and in 2016 he was diagnosed with Ankylosing

Spondylitis. Rick operates the website RADiabetes.com and he writes for RheumatoidArthritis.net. In 2018, he was appointed to both the Food and Drug Administration's Patient Advisory Council and the Arthritis Foundation Patient Engagement Committee. Rick holds Bachelor and Master's degrees from Indiana University and a Doctor of Education from Nova Southeastern University in Ft. Lauderdale, FL.

Jean Roberts is a retired scientist and 25-year resident of Hamilton County. Jean manages a band called *Blackberry Jam - The Folk Band*, which performs in Noblesville and central Indiana. Jean volunteers with Pioneer Village at the Indiana State Fair.

Writer **Ellen Santasiero** loves living, writing, and teaching in central Oregon. She teaches literature and creative writing at Oregon State University and memoir and environmental writing classes at other venues. Her writing has appeared in *The Polk Street Review, The Sun, Northwest Review, thestayproject, Oregon Humanities, High Desert Journal,* and in *Going Green,* an anthology from the University of Oklahoma Press, among others. She grew up in New York and Indiana.

Bonita Cox Searle is an Indiana native, poet, and writer who has lived in Noblesville for 20 years. Her work has appeared in *Flying Island, Indiana Voice Journal,* and *The Polk Street Review.*

Letters, postcards, poems, family history, short stories – **Nancy Simmonds** writes them all from Northeastern Indiana. A member of the Poetry Society of Indiana, NIPOETS, and three book groups, when a pen isn't in her hand or her head in a book, she designs and sews scrap quilts, plans travel adventures, and trains for road races. She is currently 1069 miles into a 3521-mile challenge run across America.

Jansen Sovich lives in Phoenix, AZ. He is a wildlife preservation volunteer by day, artist and writer by night. Jansen enjoys creating fractal art, which is a digital form of algorithmic art, created by calculating fractal objects and representing the calculation results as still images, animations, and media. The mathematical beauty of fractals lies at the intersection of generative art and computer art, where they combine to produce a type of abstract art. Because of the butterfly effect, a small change in a single variable in the algorithms used can have an unpredictable outcome.

Bryony Stanger is new to Noblesville. Most recently, she lived and worked in Washington DC. Showing excellent timing and superior judgement, she left DC and moved to Noblesville to join her fiancée, Dalton Stewart. Bry will become Mrs. Stewart on May 4th, 2019, at the historic Forest Park Inn! She has fully embraced Dalton's hometown as her own and is deeply involved in its culture. Bry has volunteered at the last two Noblesville Preservation Alliance (NPA) Historic Home Tours and was the lovely 1890s "Bathing Beauty" riding the NPA's entry in last year's Darlington Bed Race – no doubt a significant factor in NPA's entry receiving the coveted Peoples' Choice Award! Bry and Dalton share a love of Dungeons and Dragons, and Bry developed a thriving on-line business based on the popular D & D culture. She uses her artistic vision and talent to create images of players' individual characters. Players imagine their own characters; Bry brings them to life! This gifted, completely self-taught artist is also writing and illustrating her own original comic book. Three of the book's characters, *Renn, Assassin Lvl 17*, and *Kee*, are included in this year's *The Polk Street Review*. Bry is happily employed as a Production Assistant for Kit & Kaboodle, a successful Noblesville-based scrapbooking business owned by Andrea Meyer.

Michael Stewart is a life-long resident of Noblesville, arriving as a newborn at the Harrell Hospital in downtown Noblesville. He attended grade school at historic First Ward, junior high at the old Boys & Girls Club on Conner Street, and was in the first freshman class to attend the high school built in 1961. After graduation, Mike played guitar and sang in several bands, performing in many of central Indiana's and neighboring states' finest dives. This halcyon time was interrupted by the US Army draft board. Though not his first choice, Mike was proud to serve his country for three years, including a one-year tour in Viet Nam. Mike is a retired Engineering Technical Designer. During his 46 years at HNTB, his design projects included the Noblesville Sewage Treatment Plant. Glamorous, yes, but his true passion is his music, and retirement has allowed him to devote most of his time to playing guitar, singing, composing, and recording his original songs – two of which are included in this year's *The Polk*

Street Review. Mike also serves as President of the Board of Directors for *Logan Street Sanctuary, Inc*. Mike has two sons, ages 53 and 27, and four grandchildren. He and his wife, Sandy, reside in a Victorian home on Conner Street in Noblesville. The couple has renovated three historic homes together, relying heavily on Mike's design and carpentry skills.

Sandy Stewart, née Thacker, moved to Noblesville in 1952 at age five, riding on the "Hillbilly Highway" migration of southern workers to the Firestone Tire & Rubber plant. She attended grade school at historic Third Ward and First Ward schools, junior high at the old Boys & Girls Club on Conner Street, and was in the first freshman class to attend the high school built in 1961. Sandy holds a BA from Indiana University, where she majored in fine arts with a concentration in figure sculpture. After a career in advertising and fashion retailing in NYC and Boston, she returned to Noblesville in 1982 and embarked on a 36-year career in elder services. She is retired as Executive Director of PrimeLife Enrichment, though still serves the agency in a fund development capacity. Sandy is a multi-media artist in painting, sculpture, decorative arts, miniatures, needlework, and costume design – or whatever strikes her fancy! She is delighted with Noblesville's transition from the sleepy little town of her childhood to an historically significant destination city, and is especially proud of Noblesville Preservation Alliance's (NPA) role in honoring and preserving its rich history. She is an active NPA member, serving a Vice-president of the Board. Sandy and her husband, Mike, reside in one of Old Town's Historic homes with their dog, Rumi, and enjoy being able to walk to neighborhood restaurants, festivals, and live music, especially at *Logan Street Sanctuary, Inc*! Their 1889 Victorian home has been featured twice on NPA's Historic Home Tours.

Michael E. "Maik" Strosahl was born in Moline, Illinois, just a few blocks from the Mississippi River. He has been writing since youth, but grew as a poet associating with the Indiana poetry community. His work has been published in various collections, including recently in *The Tipton Poetry Journal*, the *Bards Against Hunger 5th Anniversary Collection*, and the *Bards Against Hunger Indiana Edition*. After over two decades in central Indiana, Maik has recently relocated to Jefferson City, Missouri.

Maren Thornbury is a senior at Noblesville High School. She is active in music as a bass clarinet in the Noblesville Band and as a singer-songwriter. Maren has performed in the *Fourth Friday Young Musicians Showcase* concert series at *Logan Street Sanctuary, Inc.,* and in Guitars and Stars at Noblesville HS. She enjoys writing in all genres and plans to major in English at the University of Cincinnati, which she will attend in the Fall of 2019.

Brenda VandeWater has been a Noblesville resident since 1991. She is the wife of Steve and the mother of Allie, Luke, and Zoe. She spends her days as a project manager at a software development consulting firm. She spends her evenings hanging reading, watching movies, and cuddling with their dogs, Luna and Perry.

Steve VandeWater has always enjoyed writing and for several years was the decorative concrete columnist for a trade magazine. Only recently, however, has he turned his attentions to short stories, poetry, and songwriting. Steve is on the Board of *Logan Street Sanctuary, Inc.,* and has contributed to the previous two editions of *The Polk Street Review*. He lives in Noblesville with his wife Brenda.

Zoe VandeWater graduated Noblesville High School in 2016 and has since moved to Nashville, Tennessee to pursue a college education at Belmont University. She is currently majoring in Entertainment Industry Studies and minoring in Design Communications. After receiving her Bachelor's degree next year, she plans on staying in Nashville to continue her career path in the digital marketing realm. In her free time, you can find her writing music, reading, or spending quality time with her dog Pancake.

Ever since his mother went into labor with him in a movie theater, **Sam Watermeier** has been growing as a film fanatic, journalism junkie, literature lover, and music maven. For several years, he served as an arts and entertainment reporter for the Indy publication, *NUVO Newsweekly*. His writing appears in other print and online journals, including *The Film Yap, Midwest Film Journal, THiNK Magazine,* and *The Polk Street Review*. He lives in Broad Ripple with his lovely girlfriend, Jenn Marie, and their five kitties. *Editor's note:* Sam's memoir, *Films About Ghosts*, won the *Award of Merit* (aka, *Best in Book*) in our 2017 edition of *The Polk Street Review*.

Mark Wilkinson and his wife Cathy are longtime residents of Noblesville. Mark has contributed to every edition of *The Polk Street Review*. He is an educator at Noblesville High School and is an avid fan of IndyCar racing, IU sports, and fastpitch softball.

Celeste Williams claims Noblesville as her "hometown in-law," and *The Polk Street Review* as the friend who is always urging her to get her butt in the chair and write. She spent more than 25 years writing for daily newspapers (remember those?), and then serendipity (aka, Bryan Glover) pulled her aside and dared her to write a play. *More Light: Douglass Returns*, about Frederick Douglass and Hamilton County's historic Roberts Settlement, debuted as a staged reading at *Logan Street Sanctuary, Inc.* in 2016, then went on as a full production at Conner Prairie in conjunction with Asante Children's Theatre in 2017 and 2018. Celeste's submission to this year's *The Polk Street Review* evokes *More Light* in more ways than one. Celeste is president of the Board of Indiana Writers Center. Celeste lives in Indianapolis with her Noblesville-native husband, Greg Fisher. *Editor's note:* Celeste's poem, *Vibrations in VII*, won the *Award of Merit* (aka, *Best in Book*) in our 2018 edition of *The Polk Street Review*.

Dorothy "Dottie" Zeiss Young was born at Noblesville's Harrell Hospital August 7, 1946 to Richard and Thelma Lehr Zeiss. Dottie went to Durbin Elementary and graduated from Noblesville High School (June 1964). She graduated in June 1969 from Indiana University, with a BS degree in HPER and a minor in Art. Dottie taught Art for 39 years, 38 of them in Indianapolis Public Schools. Artist, grandmother, genealogy enthusiast, and member of Beta Chapter of Tri Kappa, Dottie serves on the boards of *Noblesville Preservation Alliance*, *Cemetery Board*, and *Hamilton County Historical Society*.

The Polk Street Review is published
by Logan Street Sanctuary Press,
a division of
Logan Street Sanctuary, Inc.
1274 Logan Street
Noblesville, IN 46060
loganstreetsanctuary.org
loganstreetsanctuary@gmail.com